AQA Religious Studies

Christianity: Ethics

GCSE

Robert Bowie

Series editor

Cynthia Bartlett

Published in 2009 by:
Nelson Thornes Ltd
Delta Place
27 Bath Road
CHELTENHAM
GL53 7TH
United Kingdom

13 14 15 16 / 10 9 8 7 6

A catalogue record for this book is available from the British Library

ISBN 978 1 4085 0456 7

Cover photograph: by Corbis/P Deliss/Godong

Page make-up by Pantek Arts Ltd, Maidstone

Printed in China by 1010 Printing International Ltd

The authors and publisher are grateful to the following for permission to reproduce the following copyright material:

Text acknowledgements: 1.3 short extracts from THE ROMAN CATHOLIC CATECHISM, Burns and Oates. English translation for United Kingdom Copyright © 1974, 1999 Burns & Oates - Libreria Editrice Vaticana. Reprinted by permission of Continuum International Publishing Group UK; extract from 'A Methodist Statement on Abortion, Adopted by the Methodist Conference of 1976. Reprinted with permission; 1.4 short extract from The Church of England 1980 statement of the Board of Social Responsibility. Reprinted with permission; short extract from EVANGELIUM VITAE by Pope John Paul II, 1995; extract from (http://www.humanismforschools.org.uk/pdfs/Abortion%20(final).pdf Reprinted with permission (www.humanism.org.uk); 1.5 extract from speech by Susannah Clark, Theology Researcher for the Evangelical Alliance. © Susannah Clark. Reprinted with kind permission of the author; 1.7 short extract from Assemblies of God, Pentecostal. Reprinted with permission; 1.9 Extract from http://www.humanism.org.uk/campaigns/ethical-issues/assisted-dying. Reprinted with permission. (www.humanist.org.uk); 2.1 short extract from November 1997 General Synod of Church of England. Reprinted with permission; 2.4 Headline 'MEPs call for a ban on cloning for food' 3rd September, 2008, The Irish Independent. Reprinted with permission; Headline 'Eight clone farm cows born in Britain and their meat could be on sale in months' Sean Poulter, Daily Mail, 6 June, 2008. Reprinted with permission of Solo Syndication; Headline 'Cloned monkey embryos are a gallery of horrors ' by Sylvia Pagan Westphal, New Scientist, 12 December, 2001. Used with permission; 2.5 short extract from Assemblies of God, Pentecostal. Reprinted with permission; short extract from Assemblies of God, Pentecostal. Reprinted with permission; 3.2 short extract from Assemblies of God, Pentecostal. Reprinted with permission; 3.5 extracts adapted from UNDERSTANDING THE PSYCHOLOGICAL EFFECTS OF STREET DRUGS produced by MIND. Www.mind.org.uk. Reprinted with kind permission; 3.5 Crown Copyright materials reproduced with permission of the controller of the HMSO; 3.9 extract re www.request.org.uk. Reprinted with kind permission; 4.1 Crown Copyright materials reproduced with permission of the controller of the HMSO; 4.2 short extract from 'Marriage and Family Issues' Church of England. Reprinted with permission; 4.2 short extract from 'Your Marriage and the Church of England' reprinted with permission; 4.4 short extract from The Church of England Synod. Reprinted with permission; 4.8 extract adapted from 'Teenager faces 13 years for racist killing of Asian' by Virkram Dodd, Guardian, Saturday, December 13, 2001 Copyright © Guardian News & Media Ltd 2001. Used with permission; 4.10 Extract from article 'Girl wins religious bangle row' The Times, 29 July, 2008. © NI Syndication. Reprinted with permission; 4.11 short extract from Assemblies of God, Pentecostal. Reprinted with permission; 4.12 short extract Jean Vanier, Il ya 40 ans, La Vie, 2005 (Translation) Reprinted with permission; 5.3 short extract from THE HITCHHIKER'S GUIDE TO THE GALAXY by Douglas Adams. Reprinted with permission of Pan Macmillan UK and Random House Inc USA; short extract from 'Intergovernmental Panel on Climate Change' Report 2007 pp 1-2. (IPCC). 5.6 The Principles of The Earth Charter. Reprinted with permission of Earth Charter Center of Education for Sustainable Development at UPEACE www.EarthCharter.org; short extracts from www.fairtrade.org.uk Reprinted with kind permission; 5.11 short extract re Tearfund, from www.tearfund.org. Reprinted with kind permission; extracts from www.christianaid.org.uk. Reprinted with permission; short extract about Cafod from www.cafod.org.uk. Reprinted with permission; short extract about Trocaire. Www.trocaire.org. Reprinted with permission; 6.2 short extract from THE BOOK OF RESOLUTIONS OF THE UNITED METHODIST CHURCH. Reprinted with permission of Abingdon Press, USA.

Scripture quotations taken from the Holy Bible, New International Version, Copyright © 1978, 1984 by International Bible Society. Used by permission of Hodder & Stoughton, a division of Hodder Headline Ltd. All rights reserved.

'NIV' is a registered trademark of International Bible Society. UK trademark number 1448790

pp8-27 top Getty/Mark Wilson; pp30-45 iStockphoto/Elena Korenbaum; pp48-64 top Alamy/ Photofusion Picture Library; pp68-90 Alamy/ Ian Shaw; pp94-108 Alamy/ Tim Graham; pp118-136 Alamy/Andrew Wiard

p8 Fotolia/ Adisa; p10(tl) Fotolia/ Mikael Damkier, (br) Fotolia/ Eric Simard; p15 Fotolia/ Andriy Bezuglov; p16 Fotolia/ Emin Ozkan; p17 iStock/njgphoto; p19 Reuters/ Will Burgess; p20(t) Photoshot /UPPA,(b) Ross Parry; p24 Fotolia/ Lisa F.Young; p25 Fotolia/ Rui Vale de Sousa; p26 Fotolia/ Lisa F Young; p27 Fotolia/ Lisa F. Young; p28 Getty/Mark Wilson;p30 Fotolia/ Philip Date; p32(tl) Fotolia/ Monkey Business (br) Fotolia/ Monkey Business; p35 Fotolia/ Anatoly Tiplyashin; p36 Corbis/Reuters/ Jeff J. Mitchell; p38 Fotolia/juggle33; p37 Getty/ Image Source; p40 Rex Features/ Albert Ferreira; p44(t) Ross Parry,(b) PA Photos/ John Giles; p46 iStockphoto/Elena Korenbaum; p27 Science Photo Library/Samuel Ashfield; p48 Fotolia/ Tomasz Trojanowsk; p51 Fotolia/ PixBox; p52 RexFeatures/ClareKendall;p55(t)Fotolia/ Stephen Sweet,(b)Fotolia/ D.Ducoure;p57(t)Fotolia/ Monika Adamczyk,(c)Fotolia/ Studio Pookini, (b)Fotolia/Terex; p59 Fotolia/Konstantin Sutyagin; p63 Fotolia/ Daniel Budiman; p65 Fotolia/ Simone van den Berg; p66 Alamy/ Photofusion Picture Library; p67 Alamy/ Ian Shaw; p70 (l) iStock/Aldo Murillo, (r) Rex Features/ Tony Kyriacou; p71 iStock/ Sean Warren; p72(l) Fotolia/SFC, (r) Fotolia/Stephen Coburn; p75 Fotolia/Govicinity; p76 Fotolia/ Galina Barskaya; p77 Fotolia/Tatyana Gladskih; p79 Fotolia/ Lotfi Mattou; p80(l) Fotolia/ Stephen Coburn, p Fotolia/ Andres Rodriguez; p81(l) Fotolia/ NiDerLande, (r)Fotolia/ Ilka Burckhardt; p82 Fotolia/Jamie Wilson; p83 (t) Fotolia/Andy Dean,(b) Fotolia/Aramanda; p87 Fotolia/Moodboard; p88 Rex Features/South West News Service; p89 AP/PAPhotos/ Mark Humphrey; p90 Getty/AFP, (r) AP/PAPhotos/ Martial Trezzini; p91 Corbis/Sygma/ Philippe Caron; p92 Alamy/Ian Shaw; p93 Rex Features/Shout; p95 Fotolia/James Steid; p96 (l) Fotolia/Aaron Kohr,(r) Fotolia/Maria Bedacht; p97 Fotolia/JLV Image Works; p98 Fotolia/Andrea Danti; p99 (l) Fotolia/Ronald Hudson, (r) Fotolia/Armin Rose; p101(tl) Fotolia/Sophia Winters,(t)Fotolia/Viv,(tr) Fotolia/Imi, (bl) Fotolia/greenstockcreative, (br) Fotolia/herreneck; p103 (t) Fotolia/Pizano, (b)Fotolia/David Watts; p105iStock/fotoVoyager;p106 Fotolia/Poco; p107 Fotolia/Franz Pfluegl; p108 (bl)Fotolia/Denis Pepin, (br) Fotolia/Magdalena Ascough; p112Rex Features/ Michael Fresco; p113 Fairtrade; p114 Tearfund, Christian Aid, CAFOD; p115 Trocaire; p116 Alamy/ Tim Graham; p118 Fotolia/ Matty Symons; p119 (l) Fotolia/ Bart Kwieciszewski, (r) Corbis/Sygma/ Bernard Bisson; p123 Fotolia/ Sarah Pett-Noble; p124 Corbis/Peter Macdiarmid; p126 Fotolia/ Yang MingQ; p127 Fotolia/ Stanislav Halcin; p136 Fotolia/Anyka; p137 Fotolia/ Gerhard Seybert; p138 Alamy/Andrew Wiard; p139 Getty/AFP.

Illustrations by Paul McCaffrey

Every effort has been made to contact the copyright holders and we apologise if any have been overlooked. Should copyright have been unwittingly infringed in this book, the owners should contact the publishers, who will make corrections at reprint.

Contents

Nelson Thornes has worked hard to make sure that this book offers you excellent support for your GCSE course.

■ How to use this book

Learning Objectives

At the beginning of each section or topic you'll find a list of Learning Objectives based on the requirements of the specification, so you can make sure you are covering what you need to know for the course.

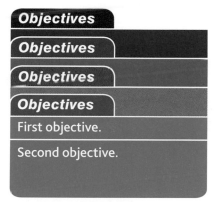

Study Tips

Don't forget to look at the Study Tips throughout the book to help you with your study and prepare for your exam.

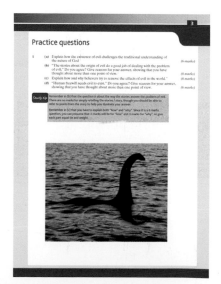

Practice Questions

These offer opportunities to practise questions in the style that you may encounter in your exam so that you can be fully prepared on the day.

Practice questions are reproduced by permission of the Assessment and Qualifications Alliance.

GCSE Christianity: Ethics

This book is written specifically for GCSE students studying the AQA Religious Studies Specification A, *Unit 2 Christianity: Ethics*. It looks at how different Christians respond to moral questions, questions of right and wrong.

You do not have to be religious or Christian to study this course. You simply need to be interested in ethical questions and what others think. You need to be willing to think deeply about your own opinions, and the beliefs and responses of different Christians. The unit will provide you with the opportunity to develop your knowledge, skills and understanding of ethics in the Christian traditions by exploring challenging moral questions.

■ Topics in this unit

In the examination you will be asked to answer questions taken from any of the topics. Topics may be mixed within questions. Chapters in this book are arranged around the topics in the unit.

The right to life

This topic examines Christian views on the sanctity and quality of life and how they influence attitudes to abortion and euthanasia.

The use of medical technology

This topic examines how Christian views on the sanctity of life, correction of nature and intervention in nature influence attitudes to fertility and genetic treatments, cloning, embryonic research including hybrid embryos. It considers who should have the right to such treatments, if anyone and what the implications are for any children involved.

Personal responsibility

This topic considers Christian views on what it means to be human, the importance of commitment and responsibility, and how these influence attitudes towards sexual relationships and the use of drugs.

Social responsibility

This topic considers how Christian views on the importance of commitment, responsibility, equality and justice influence attitudes to marriage and prejudice and discrimination.

Global concerns

This topic considers how Christian views of the world as God's creation, stewardship, justice and respect for life influence attitudes to the world and its inhabitants in relation to the environment and world poverty.

Conflict

This topic looks at how Christian views on justice, forgiveness, reconciliation and peace influence attitudes to war and peace, and to crime and punishment.

■ Assessment guidance

Make sure you can demonstrate a knowledge and understanding of different Christian beliefs and attitudes. You may need to give examples of different Christian responses, though these need not necessarily be opposing responses. Each chapter has an assessment guidance section at the end. You will be asked to mark an example for yourself – using the mark scheme below. Make sure that you understand the differences between the standard of answer for each level.

Examination questions will test two assessment objectives

AO1	Describe, explain and analyse, using knowledge and understanding.	50%
AO2	Use evidence and reasoned argument to express and evaluate personal responses, informed insights, and differing viewpoints.	50%

Levels of response mark scheme

Levels	Criteria for AO1	Criteria for AO2	Assessment of Spelling Punctuation and Grammar	Marks
0	Nothing relevant or worthy of credit	An unsupported opinion or no relevant evaluation		0 marks
Level 1	Something relevant or worthy of credit	An opinion supported by simple reason	Students spell, punctuate and use the rules of grammar with reasonable accuracy in the context of the demands of the question. Any errors do not hinder meaning in the response. Where required, they use a limited range of specialist terms appropriately.	1 mark
Level 2	Elementary knowledge and understanding, e.g. two simple points	An opinion supported by one developed reason or two simple reasons	Students spell, punctuate and use the rules of grammar with considerable accuracy and general control of meaning in the context of the demands of the question. Where required, they use a good range of specialist terms with facility.	2 marks
Level 3	Sound knowledge and understanding	An opinion supported by one well developed reason or several simple reasons. N.B. Candidates who make no religious comment should not achieve more than Level 3		3 marks
Level 4	A clear knowledge and understanding with some development	An opinion supported by two developed reasons with reference to religion	Students spell, punctuate and use the rules of grammar with consistent accuracy and effective control of meaning in the context of the demands of the question. Where required, they use a wide range of specialist terms adeptly and with precision.	4 marks
Level 5	A detailed answer with some analysis, as appropriate	Evidence of reasoned consideration of two different points of view, showing informed insights and knowledge and understanding of religion		5 marks
Level 6	A full and coherent answer showing good analysis, as appropriate	A well-argued response, with evidence of reasoned consideration of two different points of view showing informed insights and ability to apply knowledge and understanding of religion effectively		6 marks

Note: In evaluation answers to questions worth only 3 marks, the first three levels apply. Questions which are marked out of 3 marks do not ask for two views, but simply for your opinion.

Successful study of this unit will result in a Short Course GCSE award. Study of one further unit will provide a Full Course GCSE award. Other units in Specification A that may be taken to achieve a Full Course GCSE award are:

- Unit 1 Christianity
- Unit 3 Roman Catholicism
- Unit 5 St Mark's Gospel
- Unit 6 St Luke's Gospel
- Unit 7 Philosophy of Religion
- Unit 8 Islam
- Unit 9 Islam: Ethics

- Unit 10 Judaism
- Unit 11 Judaism: Ethics
- Unit 12 Buddhism
- Unit 13 Hinduism
- Unit 14 Sikhism

1 The right to life

1.1 The sanctity of life

Human rights and human dignity

In 1947, after the Second World War and the deaths of many millions of people, the countries of the world sought a new way forward, to try to prevent the horrors of the past. A small team of experts from different religions and traditions worked on what was to become the Universal Declaration of Human Rights. They wanted a statement on which all religions, cultures, belief systems and philosophies could agree. Part of this declaration includes these words:

> " *All human beings are born free and equal in dignity and rights.* "
>
> *The Universal Declaration of Human Rights, Article 1*

> " *Everyone has the right to life, liberty and security of person.* "
>
> *The Universal Declaration of Human Rights, Article 3*

All human beings have equal rights, based on the equal respect (dignity) they should receive. This is the foundation of the right to life and all other rights. This agreement reflects religious teachings of many traditions including Christianity.

What is meant by sanctity of life?

Christians believe in the **sanctity of life** – i.e., that human life is sacred. Every individual human life is precious; it has a special value beyond all price. It cannot be traded, ignored or sacrificed for some other good. As a result, the deliberate taking of a human life raises fundamental questions for Christians.

Objectives

Examine what is meant by the right to life and what is meant by the sanctity of life.

Consider how Christians apply that right in different ways.

Key terms

Sanctity of life: life is sacred because it is God-given.

Discussion activity

What do you think it means to say that life is sacred?

Beliefs and teachings

'All human life is sacred.'

Pope Paul VI, Humanae Vitae

A   *Every human life is sacred*

Why do Christians believe human life is sacred?

Christians believe life is sacred (i.e., holy and precious). There is something of God in a human person. Genesis 1:27 says, 'So God created man in his own image, in the image of God he created him; male and female he created them.' By implication, to take a human life is to kill a God-like creature, to take away a part of the image of God. God has an intention, a destiny, for every human being he created. By implication, it is not for human beings to interrupt that purpose by taking life.

Human beings have the ability to make moral decisions. They can freely do good out of love which makes them special among all other living creatures. By implication, the taking of a life ends the earthly possibilities of a loving, morally good person, and is wrong.

Christ became human and showed the possibility of perfection that human beings can aspire to be better. By implication the taking of a human life ends the possibility of a person becoming more Christ-like in this world.

Why do Christians protect the right to life?

Because of their belief in the sanctity of life, most Christians believe that the right to life should be defended and promoted.

This belief is based on central biblical teachings:

- 'You shall not murder.' (Deuteronomy 5:17)
- 'You shall love your neighbour as yourself.' (Luke 10:27)
- 'If you want to enter [eternal] life, keep the commandments.' (Matthew 19:17)

Further moral questions

Christians begin to have differences in opinion when it comes to applying that belief to real-life situations because more questions appear. If human life is sacred:

- When do we think human life begins?
  Does human life begin at conception, at birth or somewhere in between?
- Is one life more or less sacred than another life?
  If a mother's life is threatened by pregnancy, is her life less sacred than the baby's?
- Is life always worth living?
  What about a severely disabled baby born with days to live?
  What about a terminally ill person in agonising pain?

Christian beliefs about the sanctity of life affect many moral issues, including abortion and euthanasia.

Summary

You should now be able to discuss Christian beliefs about the sanctity of life and the right to life, and identify some moral questions which arise from this belief.

Activities

1. Think about the following people: a baby, an elderly person, a pregnant mother, a murderer, a severely disabled man.
2. Are all their lives equally sacred? Are they equally special, or are some people more deserving than others? Explain your view.

Activities

3. On which biblical teachings do Christians base their belief in the right to life?
4. How do you think a Christian should answer these further moral questions about applying the sanctity of life to situations?

Extension activity

Ask other people what they think is meant by the phrase 'the sanctity of life'. Compare the different answers they give. How similar or different are they from the Christian ideas discussed here?

Study tip

The Bible quotations on this page will be of use through this topic and can be applied to many of the issues discussed, such as the death penalty. See pages 136–137.

Introduction to abortion

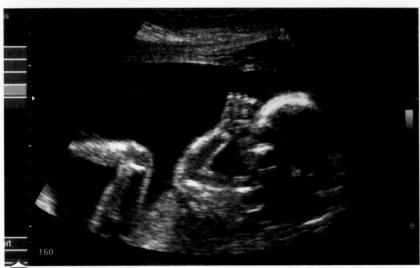

A *An ultrasound scan of a baby in its mother's womb*

What is abortion?

Abortion usually refers to the deliberate termination of pregnancy resulting in the death of an embryo or foetus (an unborn baby) through a medical procedure.

A spontaneous abortion, more commonly known as a miscarriage, is when the foetus is expelled from the womb. About one in three pregnancies ends in miscarriage. This is not a deliberate termination, but happens naturally and is often the cause of much sadness.

In the UK during 2005 there were 181,600 abortions, compared with 157,000 in 1967. Many women come to Britain seeking abortions from countries where abortion is illegal.

Abortion and UK law

In the UK, abortion was legalised by the 1967 Abortion Act. The Act was amended in 1990. Before 1967 there were as many as 200,000 'backstreet abortions'. At that time having an abortion was illegal and helping women to have abortions was also against the law. Many women were made infertile and as many as 60 a year died as a result of botched operations by unqualified backstreet abortionists.

Today, abortions are legal if:

- two doctors agree
- the point of viability (when the baby can live outside the womb) has not been reached – currently given as 24 weeks
- continuing the pregnancy would be a greater risk to the mother's future ability to have children
- it would prevent permanent physical or psychological harm to the mother
- there is a significant risk or certainty that the baby will be born with disabilities.

Objectives

Examine what is meant by abortion and the law regarding abortion.

Consider different reasons why women have abortions.

Key terms

Abortion: the deliberate termination (ending) of a pregnancy, usually before the foetus is twenty-four weeks old.

Discussion activities

1   What things might help a Christian trying to make a moral decision?

2   Look back at the quotations on pages 8–9. How might you expect a Christian to respond to the issue of abortion?

B   *Many young women who have unplanned pregnancies find themselves faced with a difficult choice. How can Christians support women in these situations?*

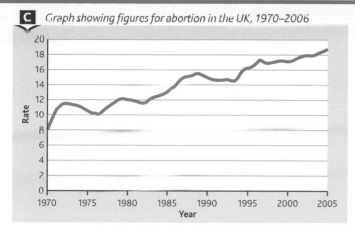

C *Graph showing figures for abortion in the UK, 1970–2006*

In practice, if a woman wants to have an abortion and the foetus is less than 24 weeks, it is usually granted. In the NHS women may have to wait some days or weeks before the abortion can take place, but private clinics can offer very quick appointments.

Abortion around the world

A few countries, such as Ireland and Spain, prohibit abortion. Those unable to travel to countries where abortion is legal may choose 'backstreet' abortions. There are estimated to be over 20,000,000 unsafe abortions of this kind every year worldwide.

How is abortion carried out?

Abortion is either medical (using drugs) or surgical (using surgery). Methods include:

- The abortion pill, which is used in the first seven weeks of pregnancy, by taking two pills, two days apart; the pills trigger bleeding and the expulsion of the foetus.
- The morning-after pill, which is taken within 72 hours of sex, either delays ovulation, therefore acting as a contraceptive, or causes the fertilised ovum to be expelled.
- Vacuum aspiration abortion: a tube is inserted into the womb through the cervix, and the contents, including the foetus, are sucked out.
- Partial birth abortion: usually used in later pregnancies if the foetus has severe foetal abnormalities, or because the mother's life is in danger. The foetus is extracted into the vagina, killed and then removed.

Why do women have abortions?

There are many reasons, including:

- as a result of a casual sexual encounter, where a child is not desired
- because it would interfere with the career or lifestyle of a person
- as the result of rape or incest
- as the result of the detection of a medical abnormality in the unborn child
- when the life of the mother is threatened by a medical condition
- among teenagers, out of fear of the parents' reaction.

 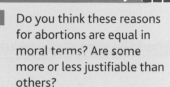

Different views on the start of life and the embryo

When does life begin?

All life comes from life. The question 'when does life begin?' usually means when does a human being (or something that will develop into a human being) become present?

The next question linked to this is 'at what point do we consider a human life form to have the right to life, the same moral status as a born human being?'

The Universal Declaration of Human Rights grants the right to life to every human being but this is not taken to extend before birth.

When is a human life form to be treated as a human being with rights?

Discussion activity

Does the moral importance of a human being come from what he or she can do, or what he or she is?

Day 1	Fertilisation – the unique genetic blueprint for the whole human being is formed.
Day 6	Implantation of embryo in uterus.
Day 14	Primitive streak is evident (forerunner to the spine and brain).
3 weeks	The heart starts beating.
6 weeks	Brainwaves are detected.
8 weeks	Kicking begins (though may not be felt until later). Some argue that at this point pain is felt.
9 weeks	Head movement.
11 weeks	Main body systems are functioning, grasping, yawning, feeling and smelling.
20 weeks	Can recognise the mother's voice.
21–23 weeks	A few babies born at this point survive. In the UK in 2005, 52 lived for more than a year.
24 weeks	Viability in UK law. Almost half of babies born at this point survive.
28 weeks	Baby is breathing amniotic fluid, moves and kicks.
34 weeks	Baby is opening and closing eyes and soon after can see the difference between light and darkness.
38–40 weeks	Birth.

 A Foetal timeline

Activities

1 When does human life become important enough to value and be given the right to life? Use the timeline to help make your decision.

- At conception, when the unique genetic information comes into existence?
- When the embryo implants in the womb?
- When the foetus 'looks human'?
- When the mother can feel the embryo or foetus move?
- When the brain starts functioning?
- When the foetus is 'viable' to survive outside the womb?

- When the foetus becomes sentient (aware)?

You may like to return to this page at the end of the chapter and decide if you still agree with your initial view.

2 a Does the foetus gradually become more human and of greater value?

b Does the point at which a foetus feels pain matter? If so why?

c Justify your decision and compare with others in your group. If you have different views, try to explore what lies behind those differences.

Christian views on the start of life and the embryo

Before birth

There is little debate that a human person exists before birth. The Bible makes reference to human life in the womb being known and called by God, and for the unborn baby to be considered as morally important.

Beliefs and teachings

'Before I was born the Lord called me.'

Isaiah 49:1

'Before I formed you in the womb I knew you, before you were born I set you apart.'

Jeremiah 1:5

'If men who are fighting hit a pregnant woman and she gives birth prematurely but there is no serious injury, the offender must be fined whatever the woman's husband demands and the court allows. But if there is serious injury, you are to take life for life.'

Exodus 21:22–23

However, there are differences among the Churches. For some Christians ensoulment, which refers to the placing of a soul in a human being, matters.

Extension activity

There has been some recent research on when the foetus is able to feel pain and also the point at which life is viable. Use the internet to search for more information about this. For instance, you could search a news site such as BBC online or Times online.

Study tip

You do not need to learn all of the different stages of development for the exam but you will need to know why certain points, such as conception and viability, are important for some Christians.

B   *Beliefs and teachings: different Chirstian views on when life starts*

All human rights at conception	When the embryo breathes	It develops throughout pregnancy
The early Church father, Tertullian (160–220 CE), wrote: 'Now we allow that life begins with conception because we contend that the soul also begins from conception; life taking its commencement at the same moment and place that the soul does.' (Apology 27) 'Human life must be respected and protected absolutely from the moment of conception. From the first moment of his existence, a human being must be recognised as having the rights of a person – among which is the inviolable right of every innocent being to life. (*Catechism* 2270)	'The Lord God formed the man from the dust of the ground and breathed into his nostrils the breath of life, and the man became a living being.' (Genesis 2:7) Some Christians use this to argue ensoulment happens when breathing begins. Before an embryo begins to breathe amniotic fluid, abortion can be justified.	'It is simply not possible to identify the single moment when a new human person begins. The right of the embryo to full respect clearly increases throughout a pregnancy.' 'There is never any moment from conception onwards when the foetus totally lacks human significance – a fact which may be overlooked in the pressure for abortion on demand. However, the degree of this significance manifestly increases. At the very least this suggests that no pregnancy should be terminated after the point when the aborted foetus would be viable.' (Methodist Church of Great Britain, 1976)
The status of the embryo		
The embryo has full human rights and should be treated like any other born human being. It is a human person.	After the embryo begins to breathe it has full human rights. Before it begins to breathe it is not fully human.	The embryo is developing towards being a full human person with full human rights. However, 'it lacks independence and the ability to respond to relationships' so is not the same. Over time it is becoming more human and so gains rights progressively. It should be treated with respect.

Activity

3   Study the table about different views on when life starts.

   a   Identify the specific difference between the Methodist statement and the Catholic statement.

   b   From these two positions, how might these Churches differ in their teaching on abortion?

   c   Which point of view is closer to your own view? What are your reasons for this view?

Summary

You should now be able to discuss when life begins, when it should have the right to life and different Christian answers to these questions.

Pro-life and pro-choice arguments

■ Christian views on when life begins

The Church of England and the Methodist Church suggest that abortion is justified when the health of the mother is in danger, or in the case that the embryo is severely deformed and may live a very short time. The Roman Catholic Church is completely opposed to abortion. Some Christians believe that an unborn baby in the early stages of pregnancy is not the same as a baby in the later stages of development and permit early abortions in certain circumstances.

■ Pro-choice arguments for abortion

Pro-choice groups argue in favour of legalised abortion. Some of these arguments may also be used by Christians who believe they follow the command to love one another.

- The right to choose: women have the right to choose what happens to their body so they have the freedom to live independent and professional lives.
- Unsafe abortions: without legalised abortion, there would be a rise in unsafe backstreet abortions leading to many deaths.
- Mother incapable: some women may be unable, either physically or mentally, to care for a baby, or even go through with the pregnancy; to do so would harm them and could endanger them and others.
- The life of the mother: pregnant women whose lives and health are threatened by the pregnancy should have their life and health prioritised over the embryo.
- Compassionate killing: it is more loving to abort severely disabled embryos who will not survive for long outside the womb rather than put them and the mother through childbirth and the sad decline to death of the of the child.
- Women in hardship: a poor single mother with no support and with other children to care for should be treated with compassion and permitted an abortion, rather than be forced to face increased hardship for herself and family.
- Freedom of will: Christians believe that human beings are given free will by God to take their own moral decisions. Some Christians argue that this means taking moral responsibility for decisions like abortion. It must be left up to them.

■ Pro-life arguments against abortion

Pro-life opponents of abortion suggest that:

- every human being has a right to life – 'You shall not murder' (Exodus 20:13)
- human life is sacred – 'You yourselves are God's temple … If anyone destroys God's temple, God will destroy him' (1 Corinthians 3:16–17)
- from the moment of conception, a human life is created and is a human person in the eyes of God – 'For you created my inmost

Objectives

Examine pro-life and pro-choice arguments.

Consider how Christians might argue for or against abortion.

Discussion activities

1 Would you expect a Christian to be in favour or opposed to abortion? Explain your answer.

2 What do you think a Christian should think about when deciding whether abortion is wrong or right?

Key terms

Pro-choice: slogan used for the view that women should have the right to choose whether or not to have an abortion.

Pro-life: slogan used for the view that supports the right to life of the foetus.

Beliefs and teachings

'These factors (when abortion may be permitted) include, for example: the occasion when a pregnancy may pose a direct threat to the life or health of the mother; the probability of the birth of a severely abnormal child.'

A Methodist statement on abortion, 1976

being; you knit me together in my mother's womb … your eyes saw my unformed body. All the days ordained for me were written in your book before one of them came to be' (Psalms 139:13, 16)

- there is no line that you can draw, such as 24 weeks, and say that on one side there is a human being and on the other side there isn't
- the embryo can feel pain during an abortion and suffers
- the woman may suffer great personal and emotional distress after having an abortion; abortion isn't a pain-free solution.

Beliefs and teachings

'In the light of our conviction that the foetus has the right to live and develop as a member of the human family, we see abortion, the termination of that life by the act of man, as a great moral evil … the right of the innocent to life admits surely of few exceptions indeed.'

The Church of England 1980 statement of the Board of Social Responsibility

'I declare that direct abortion, that is, abortion willed as an end or as a means, always constitutes a grave moral disorder, since it is the deliberate killing of an innocent human being.'

Pope John Paul II, Evangelium Vitae, 1995

'Abortion is still immoral and sinful.'

Assemblies of God, Pentecostal

'Because every foetus has significance, the abortion decision must neither be taken lightly nor made under duress.'

A Methodist Statement on abortion, The Methodist Council of Great Britain, 1976

A *An expectant mother and child*

Alternative perspectives

Humanists have concluded that abortion is often a morally acceptable choice to make. They do not think life is sacred but do think that life should be respected.

> 66 *This choice is personal; the law does not impose abortion on anyone who does not want one or want to perform one. Humanists value life and value happiness and personal choice, and many actively campaigned for legalised abortion in the 1960s … [H]umanists tend to think that a foetus does not become a person, with its own feelings and rights, until well after conception.* 99

British Humanist Association, A Humanist Discussion about Abortion, 2007

Study tip

Remember that Christians are divided on the issue of abortion. The exam might expect you to be able to explain fully two very different Christian responses to abortion.

Extension activity

Compare the different moral positions in the quotations on this page. How do they differ from each other?

Activities

1 Prepare two Christian arguments, one for abortion and one against abortion. In each case try to bring in Church teachings or Bible quotations, linked to three strong arguments on each side.

2 Having considered the two Christian perspectives, which, if either, do you think is more convincingly 'Christian' and why?

3 Reconsider your own view on abortion. Do you think you might change your mind? Which of the arguments on this page gives you most reason to reconsider your own view?

Summary

You should now be able to discuss pro-life and pro-choice arguments and identify Christian views on both sides.

Alternatives to abortion

■ A Christian duty to care for women in crisis

Many women who have abortions are single mothers. Many Christians argue that more can be done to support these women, so that they have their babies. They argue that Christians must face their responsibility to look out for the needs of these vulnerable women, offering financial and emotional help.

There are many ways in which people considering abortion may be helped to have the baby:

- through direct social and financial support from the Church community
- in cases where a teenager is involved and there are family difficulties, the Church can help to counsel parents or the young mother-to-be and bring the sides together
- by accepting and welcoming single mothers fully into Church life
- through offering fostering provision temporarily if the mother is unable to care for the child at the present time
- adoption in extreme cases where the mother cannot adequately care for and love the child.

Beliefs and teachings

'Speaking as a woman, I don't believe for a second that anyone takes the decision to have an abortion lightly ... Being part of God's family means that we look out for the needs of everyone ... If we really are part of the body of Christ and if we really believe in the sanctity of life, that has to involve us offering time, emotional care and financial help to women who need it.'

Susannah Clark, Public Theology Researcher for the Evangelical Alliance

A *Women with unexpected pregnancies may face genuine difficulties*

Objectives

Examine the alternatives to abortion.

Consider why Christians might feel they have a duty to support and care for women in crisis.

Apply your knowledge of Christian beliefs and attitudes to particular situations.

Discussion activity

How might people be supported so that they do not have to go through with an abortion?

Activity

1　Create an action plan for a local church to provide support for women in crisis. Identify the aims of the plan and how the different aims might be fulfilled. Indicate any necessary resources, human or material.

Extension activity

1　Find out about the work Christian adoption agencies do to support women with unexpected pregnancies.

Scenarios to consider

A) Jenny

Jenny is 15. She was raped by her uncle. On the face of things the extended family is very happy. Her uncle is a great friend of her father. She feels that she must get emergency contraception (the morning after pill). She feels she could never tell her family the truth and could never have the baby, even by pretending it is someone else's, knowing how it began.

B) Sarah

Sarah is 27. She is single but has three children from an earlier relationship when she was a teenager. She lives in council accommodation. She is 22 weeks pregnant but the father of the child has disappeared. Sarah finds it very difficult to make ends meet. The family live in poverty. The older children have started to get into trouble at school and with the police. She is trying to hold down a job and is encouraging them to take education seriously. She is worried about her middle child, her daughter, who she thinks may see getting pregnant as a way of getting her own place to live, and who is hanging around with some older boys.

C) Collette

Collette is 41, married and is 24 weeks pregnant. She has been suffering from pre-eclampsia (which is a medical condition where hypertension arises in pregnancy). Her blood pressure is dangerously high with the pregnancy, and the doctors have told her there is a chance she will die if she goes ahead with the pregnancy. They have advised her to have an abortion. She is a Christian and is uncertain what to do.

D) Jessica

Jessica is 20. She is at university studying a degree. She has found out that she is 3 weeks pregnant after a one-night stand with another student. They are not in a serious relationship. She is training to be a doctor and feels that having a baby now will stop her succeeding in her ambitions. Her family are very committed Catholics and they don't know that she is not a virgin.

B *Adoption is a viable alternative to abortion*

Activities

2 Read these scenarios and make a note of your own initial response to them. Discuss your responses with a partner.

3 Either working alone in pairs or in a group:

a Look at the alternatives to abortion suggested in this section. How relevant might they be to these three situations?

b Remind yourself of the different arguments for and against abortion and in particular the Christian beliefs about abortion. How might a Christian advise each of these women? Write an account of what might actually be said to these people, considering their particular situation. Make reference to Christian teachings where appropriate.

Summary

You should now be able to discuss the alternatives to abortion and why Christians might feel obliged to offer support for women in crises. You should be able to apply Christian beliefs about abortion to different situations.

Extension activity

2 Find out about organisations that support women in crisis situations, such as women's refuges.

Study tip

Make sure you can give specific and well-considered alternatives to abortion, using biblical quotations and church statements to support the different viewpoints.

What is euthanasia?

Many people suffer at the end of their lives. They may become disabled physically or mentally, and may feel a lot of pain. It can be extremely distressing for close friends and family members.

Euthanasia is often defined as the act of killing someone painlessly, especially to relieve suffering from an incurable illness. It can be done actively, which means that something is done to the person to end their life, such as giving them a lethal injection. It can also be done passively, meaning that something necessary for life is not done to the person, for instance not giving them food or water. The word euthanasia means an 'easy or good death'. It is sometimes called mercy killing.

When it involves the assistance of another person it is known as assisted suicide and if that person is a doctor it is known as physician-assisted suicide.

Why do some people want euthanasia?

It is assumed that people want euthanasia because of being in terrible pain, but according to some surveys, less than a third of requests for euthanasia are because of this. Two other reasons are also given.

Firstly, the loss of **quality of life**. Terrible physical illnesses can lead to conditions like incontinence, constant nausea and vomiting. Some people are unable to swallow or suffer complete or increasing paralysis.

In addition there are psychological factors which lead people to ask for an end of their life. They can be the result of serious depression, fear about the loss of quality of life which the illness may bring, or a sense of being an unbearable burden on others.

> 66 *Our vision is to secure the right for everyone to be able to die with dignity at the end of their life.* 99
>
> Voluntary Euthanasia Society

> 66 *When I am dying, I should like my life to be taken out under a general anaesthetic, exactly as if it were a diseased appendix. But I shall not be allowed that privilege, because I have the ill-luck to be born a member of homo-sapiens rather than, for example, [a dog or a cat].* 99
>
> *Richard Dawkins*, The God Delusion, *2006, p357*

Euthanasia in the UK

In the UK, before the Suicide Act 1961, it was a crime to commit suicide. A failed attempt could lead to prosecution and imprisonment. Euthanasia is still against the law in the UK and in most parts of the world. The law prevents doctors from deliberately taking a person's life to relieve suffering. UK law allows doctors to:

- give a powerful painkiller to a terminally ill patient who is suffering even if, as a secondary effect, the person dies sooner withdraw medical treatment if they judge that recovery is not possible. This may involve turning off a life support machine. In some cases it has been possible to withdraw food and water.

In 2006 the Assisted Dying Bill was rejected by the House of Lords. It would have allowed terminally ill people to be helped to die.

A   *For a short period euthanasia was legal in the Northern Territory in Australia. This euthanasia machine was used to kill four people*

Case study

Euthanasia in the Netherlands

Euthanasia is practised in the Netherlands. Doctors may practise euthanasia if they follow certain guidelines. These are:

- the patient makes a voluntary request
- the request must be well considered
- the wish for death is durable
- the patient is in unacceptable suffering
- the physician has consulted a colleague who agrees the proposed course of action.

It is not a requirement that the person is dying or that they are experiencing physical suffering. A first injection makes the person unconscious, a lethal injection then follows.

Activities

3   Explain what is meant by the word euthanasia.

4   Is giving painkillers which shorten life euthanasia by another name or is the main intention of alleviating pain what really matters?

5   Compare the situation in the UK and the Netherlands (see above). Which in your view is a better approach? Explain your reasons.

6   If you were to try to campaign for change in euthanasia's legal situation in either the UK or the Netherlands, what would be your argument?

Summary

You should now be able to discuss euthanasia with reference to the legal situation in the UK and elsewhere and use some of the key language associated with it.

Voluntary and non-voluntary euthanasia

Voluntary euthanasia

Voluntary euthanasia is when a person wishes to die and asks for help in doing so. This help may include providing medicines or a lethal injection to make sure that it is done quickly and painlessly. Organisations campaigning for euthanasia argue that expert advice is needed to prevent unnecessary suffering or terrible mistakes being made.

Case study

The case of Diane Pretty (2002)

Diane Pretty wanted a doctor to help her to die. She had motor neurone disease, which gradually destroyed her muscles while leaving her mind sharp. It was difficult for her to communicate. She was wheelchair-bound, unable to control her bladder, and fed through a tube. Diane had every possible medical treatment for her disease.

Diane wanted a doctor to help her die once she was no longer able to communicate with her family

and friends. Her husband Brian was desperate not to lose her, but said he wanted her to have the good death she wanted with an opportunity to say goodbye to her friends and family at home.

Diane was not able to take her own life and she did not want her husband to face prosecution by being involved. She went to court to ask for legal assistance, seeking the right to choose the time of her death with medical help, but lost the case. Diane died in a hospice in May 2002.

A   *Diane Pretty*

Because Christians hold life to be sacred, the taking of life is always a questionable act in Christian moral thinking:

- Christian teachings are against the taking of life, e.g. 'Do not commit murder'.
- Jesus brought healing and life to people, not death.
- Many Christians accept that suffering is part of what it is to be a follower of Christ. Christ suffered and died and Christians may be called to do that.

On the other hand there are those who think helping people who are suffering to die is a way of showing love and mercy and Jesus taught 'blessed are the merciful' (Matthew 5:7).

Key terms

Voluntary euthanasia: when a terminally ill person asks a doctor or a friend to help them die peacefully and with dignity. It can be called 'mercy killing' or 'assisted suicide'.

Case study

Legal grey areas

a) The Bland case (1993)

Tony Bland (aged 17) was severely brain damaged after the 1989 Hillsborough Football Stadium disaster. His parents and the hospital asked permission to withdraw the artificial food and water that was keeping him alive. The High Court and House of Lords agreed.

b) Dr Arthur's case (1985)

A Down's syndrome baby was rejected by the mother soon after birth. Dr Arthur gave the baby a sedative to stop the child wanting anything to sustain life. The child was given water but no food, and died after two days. Dr Arthur said his purpose in giving the drug was to reduce suffering. He was charged with murder and attempted murder, but was acquitted by the jury.

B   *Tony Bland*

Involuntary euthanasia (non-voluntary)

Involuntary euthanasia is when a person's wishes cannot be given for some reason, such as being in a coma, or unable to make a decision or express an opinion. In these circumstances it is someone else who has to decide to end a life for that person.

Living wills

Although they are not legally recognised in the UK, some people write 'living wills' which detail their wishes in the event that they are left incapacitated, in a coma, terminally injured and unable to express their wishes themselves. This may express their desire not to be resuscitated and not to have life-saving treatment in certain situations.

> 66 *where there are no dependants who might exert pressure one way or the other ... So long as the patient is lucid, and his or her intent is clear beyond doubt, there need be no further questions.* 99
>
> The Independent, *March 2002*

Christian responses to involuntary euthanasia vary

Christians have different responses to involuntary euthanasia. Some are opposed:

- If it involves the removal of water or food, some Christians argue that this is the same as killing. It is no different from not feeding a baby, for instance.
- Involuntary euthanasia may lead to the killing of a person against their will for some social or medical justification. For instance, the Nazis killed disabled people because they were thought to be of no 'use' to society.

Beliefs and teachings

'Intentional euthanasia, whatever its forms or motives, is murder. It is gravely contrary to the dignity of the human person and to the respect due to the living God, his Creator.'

Catechism 2324

'The Salvation Army believes that euthanasia and assisted suicide undermine human dignity and are morally wrong regardless of age or disability.'

The Salvation Army

'There is a real possibility that terminally ill people may feel pressured to ask for an early death to avoid feeling a burden to their family or the health system.'

Church of England statement on Assisted Dying Law

'The Assemblies of God condemns as immoral the killing of the weak, the physically challenged, the mentally ill, or the aged, whether by a deliberate act or by coercing or assisting a person to commit suicide. God is both the giver of life and the arbiter of life ... Humans are not empowered to take their own lives or the lives of others.'

Assemblies of God, Pentecostal

Other Christians believe that in some situations, where the person is brain dead, or in a permanent coma, it may be more compassionate and loving to allow the family to begin the grieving process and disconnect the life support machine.

Discussion activities

1. What is the difference between helping someone who wants to die and ending the life of someone who cannot speak for themselves?

2. Consider the three case studies on these pages.

  a Should Diane Pretty have been given permission by the court to decide the time of her death?

  b Was it right for the court to withdraw food and water that was keeping Tony Bland alive?

  c Was it right that Dr Arthur was acquitted?

     In each case give reasons for your answers.

Extension activity

Find out more about euthanasia cases using the internet. Use a search engine or online news site to search for the following: Dr Cox, Sue Rodriguez, Mr 'C', Kelly Taylor, Rosemary Toole Gilhooley, Dan James.

Study tip

While you will not be expected to be able to recount specific cases, knowledge of these examples will help you understand and explain some of the issues.

Summary

You should now be able to explain with examples the difference between voluntary and non-voluntary euthanasia and Christian responses to both.

Active and passive euthanasia

- **Active euthanasia** is where something is actively done to end a person's life. For instance, pills are taken or lethal injections given which stop the person's heart, causing them to die.

- **Passive euthanasia** is where something that could be done to prolong life, isn't done. This hastens a person's death. This could include not giving medical treatment, or withdrawing food and water.

- Some argue that there is no moral difference between active and passive euthanasia because the intention is the same, to bring about a person's death. Others say that actively taking a life is not the same as allowing them to die without acting, as one involves a positive action.

Activity

1   A person is visiting a terminally ill friend who wishes to be helped to die. During the visit the sick person's breathing becomes irregular and they lose consciousness. Now consider these two endings:

a   The visiting friend sees from the machine that the sick person's heart is failing. He knows he could raise the alarm and the nurses would rush in to change the medicine but he waits until the life signs on the machine stop, and the sick friend dies.

b   The visiting friend sees from the machine that the sick person is very weak. They seem calm. The friend takes a pillow from the next bed and gently places it over the sick person's mouth and waits until the life signs on the machine stop, and the sick friend dies.

Is there any moral difference between what the visiting friend does in (a) and (b)? Explain your answer.

Christian responses to active and passive euthanasia

The questions raised by active and passive euthanasia generate different Christian responses.

The interests of others

Firstly, both are concerned with a third person's involvement in the ill person's situation, be they a doctor or friend. The morality of euthanasia is not restricted to the wishes of the suffering person, but those who are also involved in that situation and whatever they choose to do. This then extends to how those choices affect people. Will they feel guilty for having helped a suffering relative? Will a doctor or nurse feel compromised by helping people to die, rather than healing?

The morality of action and inaction

Some commands suggest that moral action is most important in deciding what is right. Most of the commandments are like this. 'Do not commit murder' is not the same as 'do everything you can to help'. But is it close?

Objectives

Examine the differences between passive and active euthanasia and Christian responses to them.

Key terms

Active euthanasia: the ending of a life by a deliberate action, such as by giving a patient a fatal injection.

Passive euthanasia: allowing a terminally or incurably ill person to die by withdrawing or withholding medical treatment that would only prolong the suffering and have no real benefit.

Discussion activity

1   Can an act be morally equal to a failure to act? Suggest a situation where you think this is the case.

Beliefs and teachings

For you created my inmost being; you knit me together in my mother's womb. I praise you because I am fearfully and wonderfully made; your works are wonderful, I know that full well. My frame was not hidden from you when I was made in the secret place. When I was woven together in the depths of the earth, your eyes saw my unformed body. All the days ordained for me were written in your book before one of them came to be.

Psalms 139:13–16

Activity

2   How is this passage from Psalms 139 relevant to a discussion about euthanasia?

Christians recognise that moral behaviour is not just about what we do but also what we do not do. Jesus' parable of the good Samaritan (Luke 10:25–37) is a story about a man who is attacked and robbed and left for dead by bandits and the three people who come across his bleeding body. Two ignore him and one stops to help. It is not only that the Samaritan is good because he acted to help the injured man, but also that the others were wrong for not helping. That is how Jesus defined loving your neighbour.

The limits of mercy

Many Churches see that there can be a point where any further attempts at treating a sick person do more harm than good. When death is near, excessive treatments should not be given at all costs.

Some Christians believe that in some cases giving appropriate painkillers can hasten death. Here the 'double effect' rule allows a person to be given strong painkillers because the intention is to relieve pain. The shortening of life is a secondary effect.

Discussion activity

2   You are walking by a river and see a person in the water in distress waving for help. Do you throw the life-ring or ignore the person? If you do not throw the life-ring, are you just as bad as if you had thrown them into the river yourself?

How can this situation be used to understand the moral issues in active and passive euthanasia?

A   *Is a failure to act a sin of omission?*

Activity

3   Consider the following moral questions: why are they important questions? Which do you think is the most important?

a   What is killing people going to do to the doctors who have to help them die?

b   How can we be sure that a person really wants to die?

c   Maybe I want to die today, but will I feel differently tomorrow? Will this possibility haunt my friend, whom I persuade to help kill me?

d   How can people stand by and not help someone suffering terribly?

Extension activity

The American doctor, Jack Kervorkian, has campaigned for a terminally ill patient's right to die and claims to have assisted many patients at the end. He was imprisoned for his activities. Use the internet to find out more about his practice of active euthanasia.

Summary

You should now be able to explain with examples the difference between active and passive euthanasia and Christian responses to both.

Study tip

Make sure you can clearly explain the difference between passive and active euthanasia.

1.9 Quality of life and the right to self-determination

The quality of life

In the euthanasia debate the quality of human life is often mentioned. People expect life to have a high quality. We expect to be healthy for most of the time, be able to move and think freely and easily, be able to remember who our loved ones are and control when we go to the toilet.

However, human beings do not all have the same quality of life. Many people live in poverty and hardship; many are disabled. Elderly people sometimes lose many of their physical and mental abilities.

At what point is life no longer worth living?

In the debate about euthanasia, the question often arises: when is life no longer worth living? What kind of life is possible for someone in a permanent state of coma? How about someone who has forgotten everyone they have ever known? What about someone who has become violent, incontinent and is screaming from constant pain? If you were watching yourself lose control of all of the things that you value as they were taken by a degenerative disease, wouldn't you want a way out?

A *Many people fear the possibility of degenerative illness in later life*

The right to self-determination

Supporters of euthanasia say that **self-determination** is part of the right to life. The right to life is not always about preserving life at all costs. The ability to decide the future is part of being free. They argue being plugged into machines without the ability to enjoy the things that matter is not a life worth living. Why keep a person alive at all costs when they want to go? Supporters of euthanasia argue that self-determination matters and that death with dignity is what many people wish for. Dignity in Dying (formally the Voluntary Euthanasia Society) is one organisation which campaigns for a choice at the end of life and a dignified death for all.

Beliefs and teachings

'Whose life is it, anyway?'

The late Sue Rodrigues, a high-profile, terminally-ill resident of British Columbia, Canada

'The right to a good death is a basic human freedom.'

John Shelby Spong

'Humanists defend the right of each individual to live by her/his own personal values, and the freedom to make decisions about her/his own life so long as this does not result in harm to others.'

British Humanist Association

Objectives

Examine what is meant by the right to self-determination.

Consider Christians' responses to the right of self-determination.

Discussion activity

1 What makes a life worth living? What do you think you could not bear to live without?

links

Look back to the Tony Bland case on page 20. In what way could it be argued that he had no dignity and no quality of life?

Discussion activity

2 In groups consider the following situations:

- total paralysis of the body
- loss of control of bladder and bowel
- loss of the ability to remember loved ones and family members
- loss of the ability to reason and think clearly.

a How would the loss of each ability or capacity change your life.

b What pleasure might remain?

Key terms

Self-determination: refers to the right to make decisions for oneself in life. It is an argument use by those who agree with voluntary euthanasia.

B *Self-determination requires serious reflection*

∞ **links**

Look back at the Diane Pretty case in page 20 and explain why the right to self-determination mattered to her.

◼ Christian responses to the quality of life and the right to self-determination

Christians and Churches are usually in favour of the right to life, believing that life is sacred. Christians also believe in the freedom to love God and to do good deeds. However, when it comes to euthanasia this can lead to two different responses:

- Many Christians oppose euthanasia because of their beliefs. They believe human life is sacred because it is made by God and made for God. It is God who gives life and only God who can take it away – 'There is no God besides me. I put to death and I bring to life …' (Deuteronomy 32:39). Some also believe that human suffering brings people closer to Christ, who also suffered.

- For some Christians, because life is sacred there should be some quality to it and a person should have a right to decide for themselves if that standard of life is too low. These Christians believe God has given human beings freedom to act and the right of self-determination. The Evangelical Lutheran Church in America in 1992 said that in some situations pain is so severe 'that life is indistinguishable from torture' and that doctors struggle to choose the lesser of two evils.

Study tip

Remember that for some, the right to life includes the right to self-determination.

Activities

1 What is meant by the quality of life and self-determination and how are the two linked?

2 Compare different Christian responses to the arguments for self-determination. Which is more convincingly Christian to you? Which do you agree with, and why?

Beliefs and teachings

'Everyone is responsible for his life before God who has given it to him. It is God who remains the sovereign Master of life. We are obliged to accept life gratefully and preserve it for His honour and the salvation of our souls. We are stewards, not owners, of the life God has entrusted to us. It is not ours to dispose of.'

Catechism 2280

Summary

You should now be able to discuss the arguments about the quality of life and the right to self-determination and express Christian responses to them.

1.10 The hospice movement

Objectives

Examine the hospice movement.

Consider how Christians might consider the hospice movement an ideal response to the terminally ill.

Discussion activity

Should our response to the suffering terminally ill be to end their life or to make them comfortable and in as little pain as possible?

■ Cicely Saunders' alternative to euthanasia

Some Christians believe that the desire for euthanasia threatens the incurably ill by trying to hasten death, rather than helping people to face up to suffering. Cicely Saunders was a doctor and a member of the Anglican Church who opposed euthanasia. She felt that the moments at the end of a person's life were just as special as any other. She believed that dying was as natural as being born and that you matter even at the last moment of your life.

> ❝ I have seen people achieve so much in the ending of their lives – times that their families would have missed. ❞
>
> *Cicely Saunders*

Key terms

Hospices: special places to which people go, to die with dignity.

Beliefs and teachings

'I have seen his ways, but I will heal him; I will guide him and restore comfort to him.'

Isaiah 57:18

The hospice movement

In 1967 Cicely Saunders founded the **hospice** movement with St Christopher's, the world's first purpose-built hospice. There are now 220 hospices in the UK and over 8000 throughout the world. In the UK 60000 people are admitted to hospices, and 120000 patients living at home are supported by hospice care. Many people dying from cancer are supported by hospice care.

The hospice

The hospice is a place where expert pain and symptom relief is combined with all-round care, to meet the physical, social, psychological and spiritual needs of patients, their family and friends. Hospices are places where patients can garden, write, talk, have a drink and get their hair done. Hospices give those nearing the end of their life comfortable, warm surroundings. Many churches and church schools support local hospices by fundraising, sending volunteers to work there and arranging visits, such as carol concerts at Christmas.

> ❝ I once asked a man who knew he was dying what he needed above all in those who were caring for him. He said, 'For someone to look as if they are trying to understand me.' Indeed, it is impossible to understand fully another person, but I never forgot that he did not ask for success but only that someone should care enough to try. ❞
>
> *Cicely Saunders*

A *Not assisted dying but assisted living*

B   *How does the work of hospices reflect Christian beliefs?*

An alternative response to the dignity of the person

Many Christians would argue that the work of the hospice movement is a much better example of a Christian response to the terminally ill than euthanasia. This is because the hospice movement:

- emphasises compassionate care with expert pain relief
- emphasises healing, if not physically then spiritually
- emphasises valuing the person and every moment of their life.

While some people are concerned with the right to choose the end of your life, hospices see the end of life as an important part of your life. Care is not just about medicines or treatments, but emotional, spiritual and psychological care. The hospice movement sees the dignity of every human person, believing that they have dignity even at the moments close to death.

Activities

1   How can it be argued that euthanasia is a failure to understand the importance of dying and death and a denial of human responsibility for the incurably ill?

2   In what ways is the hospice response different to the euthanasia response?

3   How could it be argued that the hospice movement is a better Christian response to the suffering of the incurably ill than euthanasia?

Extension activity

Find out about the work of a hospice local to you. You could even consider what support you might be able to give through your school for your local hospice.

Study tip

Remember that hospices care for both the patients' medical needs and their spiritual needs. Make sure you can explain how they do this.

Summary

You should now be able to discuss the work of the hospice movement and how it is, arguably, the most Christian response to the terminally ill.

1

The right to life – summary

For the examination you should now be able to:

✔ explain the terms 'right to life', 'sanctity of life (or life is sacred)', 'abortion', 'embryo'

✔ understand the different views on when life begins and the status of the embryo/foetus

✔ explain and evaluate Christian arguments for and against abortion

✔ explain and evaluate pro-life and pro-choice arguments

✔ outline the arguments related to the quality of life and self-determination as part of the right to life

✔ describe and explain alternatives to abortion

✔ give reasons for the arguments using biblical teachings, Church teachings and other justifications

✔ explain the terms 'euthanasia', 'voluntary euthanasia', 'non-voluntary euthanasia', 'active euthanasia', 'passive euthanasia', 'hospice'

✔ understand and evaluate Christian and other arguments for and against euthanasia

✔ describe and explain the work of the hospice movement

✔ give reasons for the arguments using biblical teachings, Church teachings and other justifications.

Sample answer

1 Write an answer to the following exam question.

'"Christians should never agree with euthanasia." Do you agree? Give reasons for your answer, showing that you have thought about more than one point of view.' *(6 marks)*

2 Read the following sample answer.

'Christians should not agree with euthanasia because the Bible has many teachings that say you should not take life. The Bible says "do not kill". Also, in the Bible, Jesus healed many people. The Bible is important for Christians, as it helps guide them in life. They should follow the rules in the Bible and also try to be like Jesus. Some Christians think that God has given them freedom to decide what they should do. They may think that helping someone who is in great pain is as a way of showing love and mercy.'

3 With a partner, discuss the sample answer. Do you think there are other things that the student could have included in the answer?

4 What mark would you give this answer out of 6? Look at the mark scheme in the Introduction on page 7 (AO2). What are the reasons for the mark you have given?

Practice questions

The right to life is the most important right of all so we should not kill.

The right to life means we should be able to choose when and how we die.

1   Explain the difference between active and passive euthanasia.   *(2 marks)*

2   'There is no need for euthanasia because we have hospices.' What do you think? Explain your opinion.   *(3 marks)*

3   Give three reasons why a woman may wish to have an abortion.   *(3 marks)*

4   'Christians should never agree with abortion.' Do you agree? Give reasons for your answer, showing that you have thought about more than one point of view. Refer to Christianity in your answer.   *(6 marks)*

Study tip   Remember, when you are asked if you agree with a statement, you must show what you think and the reasons why other people might not agree with you. If your answer is one-sided you will only achieve a maximum of 4 marks. If you make no religious comment, then you will achieve no more than 3 marks.

2.1 Artificial insemination

Fertility: a sign of God's blessing

For many Christians children are a sign of God's blessing and part of his plan for married couples.

Beliefs and teachings

'Sons are a heritage from the Lord, children a reward from him. Like arrows in the hands of a warrior are sons born in one's youth. Blessed is the man whose quiver is full of them. They will not be put to shame when they contend with their enemies in the gate.'

Psalms 127:3–5

'God blessed them and said to them, "Be fruitful and increase in number"'

Genesis 1:28

People expect and hope to be able to have children. However, some are not successful. Some fertility problems can be treated, but not all couples can have children naturally.

What fertility treatments are available?

In addition to drug treatments that are available, couples may be given advice about when they should make love and how they should make love. Many couples take more than a year to conceive their first child. There are also lifestyle issues which reduce fertility. Smoking, excessive alcohol consumption and drug use can lower fertility, so lifestyle changes can improve chances of conception. However, in cases where couples have followed advice and have still not conceived, there are other possible treatments available in the UK including artificial insemination, in vitro fertilisation and surrogacy.

What is artificial insemination (AI)?

Artificial insemination (AI) involves placing sperm into the uterus of a female to make her pregnant without sexual intercourse. It can help a woman to conceive a child when natural love-making fails.

Sperm may be provided by the woman's husband or partner (**artificial insemination by husband (AIH)**). Alternatively, donor sperm may be provided by a sperm donor who may be known or unknown (**Artificial insemination by donor (AID)**).

Christian responses to artificial insemination
All forms of artificial insemination are wrong

Many Christians would say that people do not have a right to have their own children but that they are a gift from God and only God can

Objectives

Investigate the different forms of artificial insemination.

Explore moral issues raised by artificial insemination and different Christian responses to it.

Key terms

Artificial insemination (AI): sperm medically inserted into the vagina to assist pregnancy.

Artificial insemination by husband (AIH): when a woman is made pregnant by the sperm of her husband, but not through having sexual relations with him.

Artificial insemination by donor (AID): when a woman is made pregnant by the sperm of a man other than her partner, but not through having sexual relations with him.

A *The inability to conceive can cause very great sadness for couples*

Discussion activity

Why does not being able to have children cause so much suffering? Do we have a right to have children, or are they a gift? Should nature always be corrected?

make new life. The Bible sees children as a sign of God's blessing and many Christians today see children as gifts or blessings.

Some Christians believe that new life should be the fruit of marriage, created within the loving relationship of the man and wife. They believe technology should not be used when it comes to making new life.

Artificial insemination with the husband's sperm is morally justified

Some Christians think that you can use medical technologies such as artificial insemination to help have babies, and correct nature. The Church of England teaches that it may be right if the husband's sperm is used, as this may help the couple to have the child they wish for. However, it is wrong to use donor sperm because it brings another partner into the marriage. This could harm the marriage and also the child, who may not know the biological father.

Artificial insemination with donor sperm may be morally justified

Some Christians may argue that donor sperm could be used in certain circumstances, for instance, if a husband does not want to pass on an inherited degenerative disease, but wishes to have a child related to the mother genetically, rather than adopt a child that is biologically unrelated. Christians may say this is the most loving thing to do.

Beliefs and teachings

'[T]his Synod, believing that children are a gift from God in creation and that the welfare of any child created by third party donation of eggs or sperm is of overriding importance, including the need of the child for a father: affirm marriage as the ideal context for the procreation and rearing of children ... believe that treatment should normally be given to women only during years when, under normal circumstances, they might conceive.'

General Synod of the Church of England, November 1997

'[Artificial insemination is] gravely immoral ... infringe[s] the child's right to be born of a father and mother known to him and bound to each other by marriage ... [and it] dissociate[s] the sexual act from the procreative act.'

Catechism 2376

Activity

3 Read these quotations and then answer the questions that follow:

'If God does not enable a couple to have their own children, they should accept his wishes rather than seek out "unnatural" treatments. They should just pray and trust in God.'

'Infertility is just like any other illness. Fertility treatments may offer a cure to this illness. Jesus was a healer, so Christians should see fertility treatments as part of Christian healing.'

Build an argument for each of these viewpoints.

Study tip

While some Christians take an absolute stance on all forms of artificial insemination, others are prepared to consider it in certain circumstances. Make sure you can explain these different views.

Extension activity

Have a class or group discussion about what sort of treatment should be provided by the state (for free) for people who cannot conceive naturally.

Activities

1 Consider the different Christian views on artificial insemination. Identify the different arguments used.

2 What is your opinion of the different Christian views on AIH and AID? Give reasons for your views.

Summary

You should now be able to explain the different forms of artificial insemination, discuss the moral issues raised by AIH and AID and explain different Christian responses to artificial insemination.

In vitro fertilisation (IVF)

What is IVF?

In vitro fertilisation (IVF) is a medical procedure for helping some infertile couples. The first 'test tube baby' was Louise Brown, born in 1978. Around 6,000 babies a year are now born using IVF. In IVF a woman's ovaries are stimulated to produce multiple eggs. Each egg is fertilised with sperm producing several fertilised embryos. Some are placed in the mother's womb, while others are frozen for possible later use. Those that are not used later are usually destroyed.

Objectives

Explore what IVF is and why couples want it.

Examine different Christian views about IVF.

Key terms

In vitro fertilisation (IVF): a scientific method of making a woman pregnant, which does not involve sex. Conception occurs via sperm and egg being placed into a test tube.

Discussion activity

Are test tube babies a blessing or is it sinful to want babies when they cannot be created naturally?

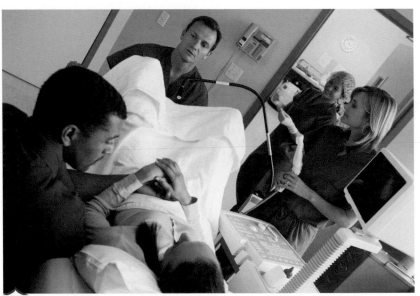

A *Doctor retrieving eggs from an ovary using ultrasound*

In some cases donor sperm or eggs are used, or a surrogate mother who carries the baby for the couple. IVF is expensive, about £2,000 per attempt, and is available on the NHS only after other treatments have been tried. Only 15 per cent of attempts are successful. For couples desperate to have children, the discovery that they cannot do so naturally can be a devastating blow. They may feel that having children is part of their purpose in life. It may be something that they have always wished for. Mothers who cannot have children can suffer depression and great sadness in their lives.

For Christians there are moral questions about what happens to the embryos that are not used, and questions about how this process might affect marriage.

Arguments for and against IVF

Christians are divided on the issue of IVF, with some deeply opposed and others in favour in some circumstances. For instance, in 1984, the Anglican Church stated that the use of embryos up until 14 days is acceptable and so IVF is permissible. On the other hand, the Catholic Church is opposed to IVF.

B *Embryologist freezing embryos for storage*

C

Arguments for IVF	Arguments against IVF
Couples should have a right to try for children. Human beings are made with the ability to reproduce. It is due to some illness or other medical problem that they cannot. This should be overcome.	Children are a gift from God and not something people have a right to have. IVF encourages the idea that children are something we have a right to have, like any other object.
Infertility is like an illness: it can cause sadness and depression, so couples should receive medical help. After all, Jesus was a healer and healed people to relieve them of their suffering. Christian love means showing people compassion and helping them.	IVF involves the destruction of new life – both the stored frozen embryos that are not used and additional implanted embryos that are not required. IVF involves killing, which is against God's law.
God asked human beings to 'go forth and multiply', so IVF is using science to fulfil God's plan by correcting mistakes in nature. Christians have a responsibility to find some way of allowing God's will to be done.	New life should come only from natural love-making and not from scientific processes. The Bible tells us in Genesis that new life should come from the coming together of husband and wife and should not involve doctors or scientists. This undermines Christian marriage.
Some Christians may argue that if no embryos are destroyed then there is nothing wrong with IVF. Destroying embryos is killing and therefore wrong, but if couples only fertilise embryos they are going to try to implant, then there is no killing.	There are many children in need of adoption. People who can't have children naturally should adopt those who don't have loving parents of their own.

Alternatives to IVF

There are other forms of fertility treatment which do not involve the separation of reproduction from the loving act in sex, and which do not lead to the destruction of embryos. There are fertility drugs and other methods which can help couples conceive, although not all couples can conceive in these other ways. For some Christians, technological possibilities may not always offer the best way forward.

Activities

1. What is IVF?
2. Why might a couple want to have IVF?
3. Read these arguments and then answer the three questions that follow:
   a. 'IVF is wrong because millions of fertilised viable eggs are chucked down the drain.'
   b. 'A child is not a piece of property, but a gift from God.'
   c. 'Children should come from making love not medical procedures.'
   d. 'Infertility is an illness which we can and should treat.'
   e. 'Everyone has the right to have children.'
   f. 'We should use science to do God's will.'
      i. Identify the strongest argument for and against IVF and the evidence used to support each.
      ii. Explain why you think they are strong.
      iii. Decide what you think.

Summary

You should now be able to explain what IVF is, what the moral questions associated with IVF are, and how different Christians might respond to IVF.

2.3   Surrogacy

Surrogacy

Some women are unable to carry their own babies. Couples in this situation may still want to have a biologically related child. This may be possible by implanting the couple's fertilised ovum into the surrogate mother who then carries and gives birth to the baby. The **surrogate mother** hands the baby back to the biological parents. This is known as gestational **surrogacy**. It is an alternative to other fertility treatments.

Surrogacy in the UK and abroad

In the UK, commercial surrogacy, in which a surrogate mother is paid a fee to carry the child, is illegal. All that can be paid are expenses. A child born from a surrogate mother can have its biological parents recognised by a court under the Human Fertilisation and Embryology Act 1990. Some countries have banned surrogacy completely, while in others, including Israel and some US states, it is legal.

Moral questions about surrogacy

There are a number of moral questions about surrogacy:

- Does surrogacy turn a woman's body and womb into an item which can be bought?
- Does it matter if a baby is born from one woman, but is then handed to another who will be its mother?
- Does surrogacy encourage the idea that we have a right to have a child?
- Is surrogacy natural or according to God's will?

Activity

1. Read these quotations and then attempt the task that follows:

   'When a women gives her womb and body to a couple wanting to have a child, she is making a sacrifice for their good. It is a Christian thing to do.'

   'Fertility treatments raise difficult moral questions but adoption is perfectly straight forward. There are many children alive today that need good mothers and fathers. The Christian option is to adopt.'

   a   Build an argument for each one of these viewpoints, drawing on information from this chapter.

   b   Which do you find more convincing?

Christian responses to surrogacy

Surrogacy in the Bible

The Bible contains examples of surrogacy. Abraham and Sarah wanted a child (Genesis 16:1–6). God had said they would have children but they were both very old. Sarah encouraged Abraham to have a baby with her servant girl, Hagar, who bore them Ishmael.

Objectives

Examine what is meant by surrogacy and why people choose to use a surrogate mother.

Explore the moral issues raised by surrogacy and evaluate different Christian responses to surrogacy.

Key terms

Surrogate mother: a woman who has a baby for another woman.

Surrogacy: a form of fertility treatment in which a woman's egg is fertilised artificially by another woman's partner or an embryo from another couple is created through IVF and then implanted into the 'host' woman. The woman carries the baby throughout pregnancy and gives it to the other couple after birth.

Discussion activity

Is carrying another person's baby an act of love, or is it wrong?

Extension activity

1. Read the story of Abraham, Sarah and Ishmael (Genesis 16:1–66). Do you think a Christian would use this story to justify surrogacy?

Some Christians may use this example to argue that surrogacy could be justified morally. Women offering themselves as surrogate mothers could argue that they are doing so just as Hagar agreed to carry Abraham's son.

However, many Christian Churches are opposed to surrogacy and do not accept that these stories in the Bible are there to offer a general moral rule, but rather they are for special cases.

Christian support for surrogacy

Christians may not use the biblical examples to justify surrogacy but they may instead believe it is a loving thing to do. Christians believe that responding to the love God gives them should involve loving responses to others. If they have been fortunate enough to have the ability to bear children, they should be able to share this gift with others who are not so fortunate. For this reason some Christians are in favour of surrogacy.

A *Becoming a surrogate mother can be a life-changing experience*

> ❝ *Becoming a surrogate mother can be a life-changing experience that brings joy and satisfaction to the surrogate mother. Surrogate mothers are not just having babies for couples who want to be parents, they are building families.* ❞
>
> *Christian supporter of surrogate mothers*

Christian opposition to surrogacy

Some Christians are opposed to surrogacy. It involves another person in the relationship between the married couple and in the act of creating new human life. Also it undermines the right of the child to be conceived, carried in the womb, born and brought up within marriage. This is important so that the child can discover its own identity and achieve its own proper human development. This is the view of the Roman Catholic Church.

Activities

2 What is surrogacy?

3 Why do some couples choose to have a baby using a surrogate mother?

4 Consider two different Christian responses to surrogacy. What reasons do Christians give for their views?

Extension activity

2 Research some true stories of surrogate mothers and people who have babies because of surrogate mothers. You could use the internet. Once you have some personal stories, reconsider your response to the issue, and the arguments made by different Christians.

Summary

You should now be able to explain what surrogacy is and UK law about surrogacy. You should be able to discuss the moral issues and understand different Christian responses to surrogacy.

2.4 Genetic engineering

Hello Dolly

On 24 February 1997, Ian Wilmot and his fellow scientists at the Roslin Institute near Edinburgh announced to the world that they had cloned a lamb named Dolly. Photographs of Dolly were on the front page of every newspaper in the world.

The genetic age had arrived with a whole new range of technological possibilities, including **cloning**, on the horizon and many other potential developments still unknown. However, there was panic. Through genetic engineering, humankind seemed to be on the verge of breaking a whole range of scientific moral taboos. In some countries there was a rush of laws to prevent irresponsible use of the new technology.

A Dolly or folly?

Key terms

Cloning: the scientific method by which animals or plants can be created which have exactly the same genetic make-up as the original, because the DNA of the original is used.

Embryo: fertilised ovum at about 12–14 days when implanted into the wall of the womb.

Moral questions

People began asking a number of moral questions:

- Would we be able to create new kinds of crops that could feed the world?
- Could we replace lost loved ones (pets or people)?
- Could we improve human beings through genetic modification?
- Would we be able to develop a whole new range of medical treatments for incurable diseases?
- Were we replacing God as creators of humanity? Is this the ultimate blasphemy?

Discussion activity ■■■

Should human beings explore every technological possibility? Are some possibilities always 'off-limits'? How should we decide which technology is moral and which is not?

Activities

1 Which of these questions concerns you the most?
2 Is the genetic age a brave new world of possibilities, or a technological nightmare – what is your initial reaction to these questions?

One response to the new genetic age has been alarm:

'MEPs call for a ban on cloning for food'

Belfast Telegraph, 2008

'Eight clone farm cows born in Britain and their meat could be on sale in months'

Daily Mail, 2008

'Cloned monkey embryos are a "gallery of horrors"'

New Scientist, 2001

Some campaigning groups have opposed the introduction of genetically modified crops and public opinion has turned against this new application of the technology even though some scientists say that genetically modified (GM) crops could help world food shortages and feed the poor in developing countries.

Misconception

Before exploring these questions it is important to put aside a misconception that is encouraged by science fiction movies. In many movies, genetic cloning is represented with the reproduction of identical fully grown human beings. At present there is no way a fully grown human being can be recreated apart from going through the usual growing-up process.

Kinds of genetic engineering

There are two important applications of the new technology which raise religious and ethical questions for Christians:

- Embryonic stem cell cloning: the use of the new technology to create new genetically identical life. This uses embryonic stem cells – taken from human **embryos**.
- Gene therapy: the use of the technology to develop new tissue cells that could be used to treat diseases. This uses adult stem cells.

A third set of issues is raised by this new technology concerned with the possibility of creating designer babies (page 42) and 'saviour siblings' (page 44).

This diagram illustrates the new technology.

- The red nucleus is the body cell with the desired genes.
- The green nucleus is undesired.
- The yellow is the egg cell.

The red (desired) nucleus is placed in the yellow egg, having removed the green (undesired) nucleus. This is a clone cell which could be implanted in a surrogate mother to produce an identical living being, or to develop tissue cultures for therapeutic treatments. This process is called somatic cell nuclear transfer (SCNT).

The somatic cell is usually a fertilised ovum. This is one of the causes of disagreement amongst Christians because such cells are considered by some to be fully valued human beings in embryo. Some scientists are experimenting with adult cells which do not require the destruction of a nucleus.

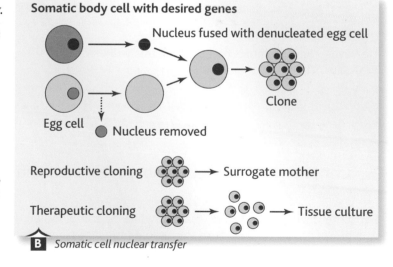

B *Somatic cell nuclear transfer*

Summary

You should now be able to discuss the moral questions raised by the new technologies in general and understand what is meant by genetic engineering.

Study tip

You will not be asked about the scientific process of the new technology but you need to understand the moral issues involved in these new developments.

Activities

3   Why do you think some Christians will be alarmed by genetic engineering?

4   What aspects of these developments raise moral problems for Christians?

Extension activity

Jeans for Genes is a national children's charity for children with genetic disorders. Find out about the work of the charity at their website: **http://www.jeansforgenes.com**.

What is embryo experimentation?

In 1990 the Human Fertilisation and Embryology Act legalised experimentation on human embryos of up to 14 days' development to help research into infertility, certain diseases passed down from parent to child, causes of miscarriage and contraception. Only spare embryos arising from in vitro fertilisation (IVF) treatment could be used. After that period the embryos must be destroyed.

Hybrid embryos

A hybrid embryo is a mixture of both human and animal tissue. Some scientists want to place human DNA in animal eggs. The result would be mostly human, with a small animal part. The hybrid embryo would be grown in the lab for a few days and would then be harvested for stem cells. Scientists could use this because there is a shortage of human eggs available for research. Animal eggs are easier to come by. They could use it to develop cures for diseases like Parkinson's disease. UK law does not allow such hybrids to be grown into human beings, and the scientists say they are only interested in the cells, not any creature which may come out of this.

> *People think we are generating some sort of hybrid animal. This is just cells, just for science. No animal is ever going to be created.*
>
> Professor Chris Shaw, *Kings College London*

However, some scientists do not think this will lead to useful research. Professor Sir John Gurdon said:

> *Scientifically ... I'm not persuaded it will work ... You could get a lot of genetic abnormality that won't lead to good-quality stem cells.*

Christian responses to embryo research and hybrid embryos

For some Christians the embryo already has the same human dignity as a person who has been born from the moment of conception, while others think the moral status of the human embryo is not established until some time after conception.

> *There are stem cells available for research from legitimate sources that do not compromise the sanctity of human life. The practice of cultivating stem cells from the tissue of aborted foetuses perpetuates the evil of abortion and should be prohibited.*
>
> Assemblies of God, *Pentecostal*

Objectives

Explore what is meant by reproductive cloning and consider the moral questions it raises.

Examine different Christian responses to embryo research and hybrid embryos.

Discussion activity

If you were asked to donate an embryo of yours for scientific research, would you agree? Why/why not?

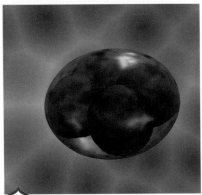

A   *A four-cell embryo: Is this a resource for science to use to bring about healing, or a sacred life which should be protected?*

Arguments against embryo research

- An embryo is a human which must be valued as highly as a human life and protected from experimentation. It should be treated as a sacred life, made by God and not something used and then disposed of. Disposing of embryos is the destruction of human life – murder.
- The embryo is an innocent human and taking innocent life is wrong. The sixth commandment says do not commit murder. Killing an innocent life is committing murder.
- The Bible encourages Christians to care for others. They should love one another, look after those who are weak and cannot protect themselves.

Additional arguments against hybrid embryos

- It is wrong to tamper with God's plan for nature. The idea of an animal human hybrid seems to go against the natural order found in Genesis 1, with animals and humans created as different creatures.
- According to the Bible, God made humans in his own image and so to mix human with animal seems to degrade the image of God.

Arguments for embryo research

- The human embryo is important, but not the same as the born human being. So, research up to 14 days is acceptable.
- Embryo research could bring medical cures which will help those who are suffering from terrible diseases. When nature goes wrong it should be corrected using scientific knowledge and developments.

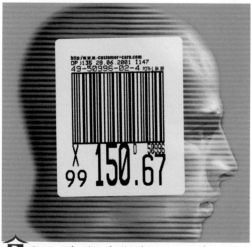

B *Is reproductive cloning human manufacturing?*

" *Genetic research conducted with reverence for life appears to have great potential for the health of human beings through the identification of and intervention in the genetic roots of hundreds of diseases.* "

Assemblies of God, Pentecostal

Activities

'A human embryo is sacred and should not be used for scientific experimentation.'

'If experimentation on a human embryo can help heal many people who are suffering now, then the research should be allowed.'

1   Consider these two views. What do you think?

2   Explain two different Christian responses to embryo experimentation giving reasons for those responses. Give your opinion about the arguments and evidence used to support these views.

Summary

You should now be able to explain what is meant by embryo research and embryo hybrids and discuss Christian responses to them.

What is stem cell cloning?

Stem cell cloning makes it possible to reproduce an identical new human embryo. A person could have a child which is their genetic identical twin (separated by a generation). In this process the existing genetic information is removed from a fertilised egg and replaced with new genetic information from the donor.

Animals have been cloned and then born in this way but it is illegal for humans in the UK and many parts of the world to be born like this. This is called **reproductive cloning** and the United Nations in 2005 said that human cloning is 'incompatible with human dignity and the protection of human life'.

However, cloning embryos for research (and destroying them afterwards within 14 days) is permitted. It is used to develop treatments for diseases and is called **therapeutic cloning**.

A   Are reproductive clones any different from identical twins?

Christian responses to stem cell (therapeutic) cloning

Many Christians from different traditions oppose stem cell therapeutic cloning.

- It involves the destruction of an embryo. Some Christians believe life from conception is sacred. Christians who are against abortion will also oppose stem cell cloning – it destroys one human life to create another. The Bible says, 'Do not commit murder' and 'Before I was born the Lord called me' (Isaiah 49:1). This argument is an argument against both reproductive and therapeutic cloning which use embryonic stem cells.

Donald Bruce (2000), director of the Church of Scotland's Society, Religion and Technology, said:

> 66 *It is my view the creation and use of cloned embryos for procedures such as these should not be allowed … I believe we should stop in our tracks, and not continue to use embryos routinely for cell therapy.* 99

Objectives

Explore what is meant by embryonic stem cell cloning and consider the moral questions it raises.

Examine different Christian responses to embryonic stem cell cloning and evaluate them.

Key terms

Reproductive cloning: the use of cloning techniques to produce a baby.

Therapeutic cloning: another term for stem cell cloning.

Discussion activity

If a child died, would it be right for the parents to have a genetically identical child recreated?

Beliefs and teachings

So God created man in his own image, in the image of God he created him; male and female he created them.

Genesis 1:24

- Babies should be created out of love, not cloning technology with scientists involved. Genesis says 'Be fruitful and increase in number … [A] man will leave his father and mother and be united to his wife, and they will become one flesh' (Genesis 1:28 and 2:24).
- Children have a right to two biological parents, a right denied them if they are a cloned child of only one parent. God intends for children to have two parents.
- This technology could lead to the creation of a master race with the rich being able to clone themselves and the poor being a second-class, 'imperfect' human race. This could also affect how we see those in society who are disabled in a negative way.

> 66 *As an Orthodox Christian, I speak out in opposition to any attempt to clone a human being because humans are supposed to be created by acts of love between two people, not through the manipulation of cells in acts that are ultimately about self-love* 99
>
> *Rev. Demetri Demopulos, Greek Orthodox pastor and geneticist*

Arguments in favour of embryonic stem cell (therapeutic) cloning

Some Christians believe that while reproductive cloning is wrong, therapeutic cloning can be justified.

- Some Christians do not believe that human life must be protected from the point of conception, but rather from some point later. The United Church of Christ Committee on Genetics acknowledges that there are possible cures which may be derived from genetic engineering. They believe the human 'pre-embryo' should be treated with great respect, but do not see it as equal to a person. They do not reject human pre-embryo research, including stem cell cloning.
- Currently scientists are allowed to use the technology for embryo experimentation. Stem cell cloning is leading to new treatments and may potentially bring cures to degenerative diseases such as Motor Neurone Disease and Alzheimer's disease.
- Though illegal in the UK and elsewhere, stem cell reproductive cloning has the potential of offering infertile couples a chance to have a cloned child, possibly using a surrogate mother.

Extension activity

Conduct a survey of other people's attitudes (other students or, perhaps, family members) towards embryonic stem cell cloning. You could ask people what they think first, then give them examples you have researched and then ask them again to see if they change their mind. Pool the answers people give you and try to make sense of them.

Activities

1. What is stem cell (therapeutic) cloning?
2. Explain two Christian responses to stem cell (therapeutic) cloning giving reasons for those responses. Give your opinion about the arguments and evidence used to support these views.
3. Compare these two views:
   'Millions of people are affected by diseases which cause mental and physical deterioration. Surely their suffering justifies the use of fertilised ova in the search for cures.'
   'It does not matter what cure you might develop or who may be helped by it, if you have to kill a person to develop it then you have done wrong.'

Summary

You should now be able to explain what is meant by embryonic stem cell cloning and discuss different Christian responses to it.

2.7   Gene therapy and designer babies

◼ What is somatic cell therapy?

Somatic cell therapy (also called gene therapy) uses adult stem cells, such as those found within bone marrow, instead of embryos. Gene therapy can be used to treat diseases, for instance organs which are not working properly. It can also help with organ transplants by making new organs compatible for the patients. Many Christians are in favour of using this technology to correct problems in nature by healing the sick.

◼ Designer babies

Many expectant parents worry that their child may be born with medical problems. Improvements in genetic engineering make it possible to check for some conditions during the pregnancy, such as the incurable genetic disease Huntingdon's disease. 'Unhealthy' embryos are removed leaving the healthy ones. If the unhealthy embryos are all aborted, the disease would be eliminated from the population.

New genetic technologies mean different features of a human person could be chosen. Parents wanting to have a baby might be able to choose or pay for particular characteristics, such as eye colour, or height and rule out medical conditions such as heart defects. This has led to the adoption of the term **designer babies**.

◼ Christian responses to designer babies

A

Arguments against designer babies	Arguments for designer babies
Designer babies may involve the selection of embryos that have the 'right' features and the destruction of those which do not. Many Christians believe that all life is sacred from conception and should never be destroyed.	Some Christians may argue that designer babies are morally acceptable when it comes to ensuring the babies are healthy. If a parent has a hereditary degenerative condition then it seems kind and loving to make sure that is not passed on.
There is a risk that the test itself could damage the foetus thus harming an otherwise human being.	The suffering of parents who give birth to one child after another who will die at a very early age is appalling. Christians would support a technique which enabled children born to fulfil their potential and parents to have the joy of watching their children grow up.
Some Christians believe that the interest in designer babies shows an unhealthy search for the 'perfect child'. New life should be accepted and loved in all its forms.	
Some Christians believe that the disabled community will be devalued by the desire to prevent all disabilities. It is important all people are welcomed and respected in society.	
Designer babies may lead to the rich becoming a better human species while the poor will not be able to afford the 'improvements'. This will divide the world and increase prejudice.	
Designer babies encourage the idea that we have a right to a baby. Many Christians believe that babies are gifts from God to be accepted and loved as they come. They are not an item to be purchased.	

> ❝ We do support pre-birth selection of embryos on medical grounds in the case of major illnesses etc. The decision to test and what to do with the results should be according to the wishes of the parents. ❞
>
> Audrey Jarvis, Chair of The Interchurch Bioethics Council (ICBC) represents the Anglican, Presbyterian, and Methodist churches in New Zealand

> ❝ We do not, as a society, have the right to initiate human life either to destroy it, or for purposes, however nobly intended, which render that life a means to someone else's ends. ❞
>
> Roman Catholic Archbishop Conti

> ❝ Another concern we have is for the disabled community. They are concerned that this type of selection will devalue disabled people. It is important that all persons, disabled or not, are valued and seen as contributing to society.
>
> This technique is fraught with ethical and clinical difficulties. It means that children will be created as biological commodities – a child as the means to another's end. There is also a considerable risk of damaging embryos through the biopsy process. ❞
>
> Roger Smith, Head of Public Policy at CARE, a UK Christian social concern charity

B   Parents may soon be able to choose their unborn child's physical characteristics

Activities

1   Would it be better to screen the population for the most dangerous of these inherited diseases to ensure that they do not have any more babies with these diseases?

2   Would the necessary abortions be worth the reduction in suffering in future generations?

Extension activity

Design a form for a designer baby clinic. What different sorts of things might people want for their child? Think about what they would want to avoid as well. Think about different aspects of a person: the physical, mental, emotional, spiritual and moral. You could then test your form on someone and then discuss what you have learnt from the activity.

Summary

You should now be able to explain different Christian responses to gene therapy and designer babies.

Study tip

Remember that Christian responses to designer babies may be influenced by whether the designed feature is cosmetic or about preventing a serious disease.

2.8 Saviour siblings

Saviour siblings

When a child is suffering from a serious condition that requires a donor who has compatible tissue for a transplant or blood transfusion, a saviour sibling can be created to help them. By creating a number of fertilised eggs, the parents of the sick child can choose one which does not have the disease and has compatible tissue – the saviour sibling. The Human Fertilisation and Embryology Authority, which governs decisions of this sort in the UK, has released guidance for future decision-making:

- The condition of the affected child should be severe or life threatening.
- The condition should be one which may continue to occur.
- All other possibilities of treatments should have been explored.
- The techniques should not be available where the intended recipient is a parent.
- The intention should be to take only cord blood for purposes of the treatment, not other tissues or organs – the sibling cannot be used as a spare parts bank.

Objectives

Investigate the moral issues raised by the possibility of saviour siblings.

Evaluate different Christian responses to these issues.

Discussion activity

Should we create a new human being to save an already existing human being?

Case study

Jamie Whitaker

Michelle and Jayson Whitaker wanted help for their son Charlie (born in 2000). Charlie had Diamond Blackfan Anaemia (DBA). This condition can only be treated with a stem cell transplant from a matched donor. However, such donors are very difficult to find from people who have a tissue match. A daughter, Emily, was born naturally, but unfortunately she was not compatible. The parents went to America, where doctors selected brother Jamie from a number of fertilised ova which were screened. Jamie was found to be a near-perfect genetic match for his older brother Charlie and he was chosen to be born. The parents went to America because it was not deemed legal in the UK.

A Jamie and Charlie Whitaker

Zain Hashmi

Raj and Shahana Hashmi have a three-year-old son, Zain, who suffers from the blood disorder, Beta Thalassaemia (BT). Zain has regular blood transfusions and may die without a bone marrow transplant. BT is hereditary and both of the Hashmis are carriers. Any child they produce carries a one in four chance of having BT. Mrs Hashmi conceived Haris naturally in the hope that he would be compatible for Zain. Haris was free of the disease but not a tissue match for Zain. His parents tried to find a donor but failed. Permission was given to carry out a genetic diagnosis on embryos from the Hashmis to find a disease-free, tissue-compatible child. Umbilical cord blood could be used to save Zain's life. Permission was granted, but the Hashmis were not successful after some failed attempts.

B Zain Hashmi

Arguments for and against saviour siblings

Arguments against saviour siblings	Arguments for saviour siblings
To get a saviour sibling many other embryos are discarded, destroyed. Christians who believe in the sanctity of human life from conception will oppose saviour siblings because of this.	Some Christians may argue that saviour siblings are no different from other kinds of blood or organ donation. It is creating someone to help another and that is morally good. Jesus, after all, healed the sick.
Creating a child to save another person means we do not value it for what it is but what it can do for another. All children should be valued for being children of God, not for what they can do.	A saviour sibling could be treated as a person as well as someone who can bring healing to another. Pregnant mothers do not exist just for themselves but for their unborn babies as well. Saviour siblings could also live for both.
Saviour siblings may be emotionally damaged when they find out they were only chosen because they could help their sibling. If they had not been lucky enough they would not exist.	Parents have more than one child for all sorts of reasons. They may want to have children who can play with each other. With saviour siblings they want a child who is capable of saving the life of a sick sibling. This is just another good reason to have a child.

> Right from the start, this child did not have the right to its own birth. The parents' thoughts were not on the birth of the child. And it lives under the threat that it might be asked for future donations.
>
> *Josephine Quintavalle, anti-abortion campaigner*

> All we are doing is trying to help someone who is sick ... All the time children are created for a reason – to complete the family, to provide a sibling for an existing child, to keep a couple together. What we are doing here is no different.
>
> *Mohammed Taranissi, director of the Assisted Reproduction and Gynaecology Unit, London*

Activities

A Christian couple, each belonging to a different Church, have a desperately sick daughter who suffers from an inherited condition, which means they need a special transplant from a compatible donor. But there is no donor available. By selecting a saviour sibling the couple could have a child who would save his or her big sister.

Ministers from each Church give advice to the couple but they have quite different views on the matter.

1. Write two imaginary letters to the couple explaining each view.
2. Alternatively you could role play the situation having prepared the sorts of thing each minister might say and how the couple might respond to what they are told.

Study tip

The exam will not ask you to recall information about specific cases but knowledge of them may help you to explain some of the issues relating to saviour siblings.

Extension activity

Two other examples of 'saviour siblings' are Jodie Fletcher and Donatella Zammit. Use the internet to find out more information about their stories.

Summary

You should now be able to explain the moral issues raised by the possibility of saviour siblings and evaluate different Christian responses to these issues.

2

The use of medical technology – summary

For the examination you should now be able to:

✓ explain the terms artificial insemination, in vitro fertilisation, surrogacy, embryo experimentation, hybrid embryos, genetic engineering, reproductive cloning and therapeutic cloning, designer babies, saviour siblings

✓ give reasons why people seek fertility treatments

✓ explain different Christian responses to different fertility treatments

✓ explain different Christian responses to embryo experimentation and hybrid embryos

✓ give reasons why people seek to have reproductive cloning and therapeutic cloning

✓ explain different Christian responses to reproductive cloning and therapeutic cloning

✓ give reasons why people seek to have designer babies and saviour siblings

✓ explain different Christian responses to designer babies and saviour siblings

✓ consider and evalate the rights of those involved.

Sample answer

1 Write an answer to the following exam question.

'Explain why some Christians are opposed to in vitro fertilisation'?
(6 marks)

2 Read the following sample answer:

'Some Christians, like Catholics, do not agree with IVF. This is because in IVF, embryos are just thrown away when they are not needed and some Christians believe that all life is sacred and the Bible says do not kill. Some Christians also believe it is unnatural to have doctors involved in making babies because God means for people to have babies by making love naturally.'

3 With a partner, discuss the sample answer. Do you think there are other things that the student could have included in the answer?

4 What mark would you give this answer out of 6? Look at the mark scheme in the Introduction on page 7 (AO1). What are the reasons for the mark you have given?

Practice questions

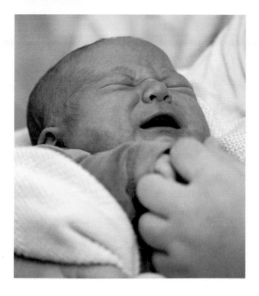

1   Explain briefly what is meant by artificial insemination.   *(2 marks)*

2   Explain Christian attitudes to the use of fertility treatments.   *(4 marks)*

3   'Christians should support the idea of saviour siblings.' What do you think? Explain your opinion.   *(3 marks)*

4   Explain Christian attitudes to cloning.   *(4 marks)*

5   'Embryo stem cells should be used to help develop cures to terrible diseases.' Do you agree? Give reasons for your answer, showing that you have thought about more than one point of view. Refer to Christianity in your answer.   *(6 marks)*

> **Study tip** Make sure you learn clear definitions for the key words. Questions about medical/scientific issues can be quite confusing so make sure you know what the key terms mean and can explain them clearly.

3.1 Human sexuality and sexual relationships

■ Human sexuality

Human sexuality can be described as how people experience sex and express themselves as sexual beings. This chapter is concerned with social attitudes to different kinds of sexual behaviour and, particularly, with Christian views about sex and relationships.

Christian views on commitment, sex and marriage

Traditionally Christians regarded sex as part of the commitment a couple makes to one another in marriage. It is linked both to the union of marriage and the life-giving aspect of it: Genesis says that a man and a woman should be united together and that they should 'go forth and multiply'. As a result, Christians have traditionally been suspicious of sexual activity outside a marriage, and some remain deeply opposed to homosexuality and artificial contraception. Others believe that Christian faith means finding the loving thing to do in the modern world, which might mean breaking with tradition.

In fact the very earliest Christians had a particular view of sex which was connected to their belief that Jesus' Second Coming and the end of the world was going to happen any day. Because Jesus did not marry, these early Christians believed that being celibate (not having sex, not marrying) was the best way to be in the last days of the world. As the religion developed, attitudes changed.

A *Shouldn't religion keep out of the bedroom?*

'Now to the unmarried I say: it is good for them to stay unmarried, as I am. But if they cannot control themselves, they should marry, for it is better to marry than to burn with passion.' (1 Corinthians 7:8–9) St Paul seemed to suggest that marriage was necessary for controlling sexuality.

Objectives

Consider key themes of Christianity and human sexuality.

Key terms

Human sexuality: how people express themselves as sexual beings.

Age of consent: the legal age for sex to be treated as by agreement.

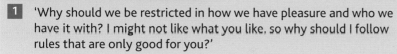

1 'Why should we be restricted in how we have pleasure and who we have it with? I might not like what you like, so why should I follow rules that are only good for you?'

'The custom in many parts of the world has been for men and women to get married and have children in that order. Life would be much more stable if everyone followed these rules.'

'Sexuality is much more complicated than some people think. It's about time we realised that it's not just about pleasure or having babies, and we need to stop trying to put people into boxes, or giving them labels.'

Discuss these three viewpoints. Do you agree or disagree with them? Explain your thinking.

2 Consider the section 'sexuality in the modern world'. To what extent do you agree with these views?

> 66 *Let me kiss him with the kisses of his mouth – for your love is more delightful than wine.* 99
>
> *Song of Solomon*

Sexuality in the modern world

The availability of artificial contraception and the legal access to abortion, coupled with greater freedom, has meant that people have felt far safer about having sexual relationships outside marriage than in the past. Some feel that sexual behaviour, of any kind, is permissible between people who freely consent. However, most people have very strong views that sexual infidelity (unfaithfulness) is wrong.

UK law and sex

In England and Wales the **age of consent** for homosexual, heterosexual or bisexual men and women is 16 years old, and has been since 2000. A person gives consent if he or she freely agrees to have sex, and has the freedom and capacity to make that choice. In the eyes of the law, sex with someone not yet 16 is sex with 'a minor', and someone of 16 or above having sex with a minor can be convicted of statutory rape or sexual assault. Children under 13 are protected by additional specific laws and not knowing the age of a child is not a defence against the charge of statutory rape.

Summary

You should now be able to explain traditional Christian views of the relationship between commitment, marriage and sex and the Christian idea of celibacy.

Extension activity

Some religious orders require members to be celibate. This is true of most Roman Catholic and Orthodox orders and some other Christian groups as well as some religious orders in other religions. Find out more information about a celibate religious order using the internet.

Study tip

The Christian belief that sex is part of a committed, loving relationship, and brings new life into the world, forms and influences Christian attitudes to many issues related to sex.

Heterosexuality and homosexuality

Understanding sexuality

Sexuality is now considered to involve many aspects of the human personality throughout life, not simply the sexual organs. Love-making affects many aspects of a couple's relationship, not just pleasure, affection and reproduction. Some argue that it is a mistake to try to label types of sexuality, e.g. **homosexual** or **heterosexual**. The media often focus on beauty and physicality, and yet sexuality and sexual relationships are, perhaps, more about affection and intimacy.

Christianity and heterosexuality

Most sexual relationships are between men and women. Biologically, this is how new life is created. Many cultural traditions assume heterosexuality is normal, so marriage rites have traditionally been presumed to be between a man and a woman. Traditionally, many cultures have been dominated by male power (patriarchy) and so women have not had the same freedoms in their relationships with men. In the modern world the idea of equality between men and women in relationships is seen to be much more important. However, traditions which suggest women are inferior remain. For instance, in marriage the father often 'gives away' the bride to the husband. Some see this as a nice tradition, while others think it reinforces inequality by showing that a woman is handed over from her father to her husband.

Christianity and homosexuality

It is thought that as many as 10 per cent of people are homosexual, i.e. attracted to members of the same gender. There are many debates about homosexuality within Christianity. Some see it as a natural part of humanity while others think it is sinful and wrong.

There is much discrimination and prejudice towards homosexual people throughout the world. In the UK in recent years the position of homosexual people has been strengthened in society due to changes in law. First, homosexual acts are no longer regarded as crimes, and legal recognition of homosexual relationships has recently been provided. Public attitudes are changing, and there is more acceptance of differences among people, although religious views on this issue differ.

Objectives

Examine moral questions about heterosexuality and homosexuality and evaluate Christian responses to them.

Key terms

Homosexual: to be attracted to a person of the same sex.

Heterosexual: to be attracted to a person of the opposite sex.

Discussion activity

1   Does being a Christian mean being heterosexual?

Beliefs and teachings

'Whatever you did for one of the least of the brothers of mine, you did for me.'

Matthew 25:40

Discussion activities

2   Why do you think equality is important in relationships?

3   Why are labels sometimes dangerous?

A

Christian responses to heterosexuality	Christian responses to homosexuality
Many Christians believe that heterosexual relationships are part of God's plan for men and women in the world.	Some Christians believe that homosexuality is a result of sin. It goes against God's plan for humanity and is forbidden in the Bible:
Genesis 1–2 describes God making man and woman as partners for one another so that they would not be lonely. Many Christians believe this when they read in Genesis that God made man and woman so that they would come together and be united with one another. Men and women are different but they complement one another and so make for a good partnership.	'God made Adam and Eve, not Adam and Steve.' (Anon)
	'Do not lie with a man as one lies with a woman, that is detestable.' (Leviticus 18:22)
	'Homosexual behaviour is sin because it is disobedient to scriptural teachings … contrary to God's created order for the family and human relationships … [and it] comes under divine judgment.' (Assemblies of God, Pentecostal)
Some Christians see Jesus as supporting this teaching in the Old Testament. For instance he performed a miracle at the wedding of Cana, turning water into wine.	Some Christians believe gay and lesbian people are not sinful because of their attraction to members of the same sex, but that sex is only for married men and women. The Roman Catholic Church teaches that gay and lesbian people are called to be celibate.
For most Christians a sexual relationship between a man and woman should be part of a loving, faithful, committed relationship.	The Church of England encourages gay and lesbian Christians who cannot live celibate lives to be welcomed in Church.
For some Christians, heterosexual relationships are the way God has intended new life to be brought into the world, with a father and a mother being able to provide different gifts and talents in the raising of children.	'[T]he Church did not want to exclude from its fellowship those lay people of gay or lesbian orientation who, in conscience, were unable to accept that a life of sexual abstinence was required of them and instead chose to enter into a faithful, committed relationship.' (Church of England)
Some Christians see a heterosexual relationship as one in which the man is head of the family, over the wife. This can be seen to mean that the man will be the one who has a job, or takes leading roles in Church, while the woman is head of the home and responsible for raising children.	Some Christians believe that many Bible texts are misinterpreted or misunderstood and that homosexuality is a part of a gift of creative variety that God has given humanity. Loving, faithful, committed homosexual relationships are just as holy as heterosexual ones:
	'I realised that my sexual orientation was permanently and purposely formed in my mother's womb or in my earliest infancy … Now I accept my sexual orientation as a gift from my loving creator.' (Mel White, gay Christian)

 Gender symbols

Summary

You should now be able to discuss moral questions about homosexuality and heterosexuality and evaluate Christian responses to them.

Extension activity

The Worldwide Anglican Communion is divided over the issue of homosexuality. Use internet news sites such as BBC News Online and Times Online to find out more about the ongoing arguments.

Study tip

Remember that within Christianity there are strong differences of opinion over the issue of homosexuality. Make sure you are able to explain the different responses to it.

Chastity and avoiding sexual immorality

Many people live together without getting married, or before getting married. But many Christians think these attitudes are wrong. **Chastity** means acting modestly and being in control of sexual urges and desires. Many Christians believe that outside marriage one should live chastely, with sexual restraint. Sex is for marriage and is not a casual or passing arrangement. This includes single people who have never been married, widows and homosexual couples.

- **Sex outside marriage** is described in the Bible as sexual immorality. It is a sign of sin (Matthew 15:19). Many Christians believe sexual immorality includes pornography, prostitution and rape.

Beliefs and teachings

'For you know what instructions we gave you by the authority of the Lord Jesus. It is God's will that you should be sanctified: that you should avoid sexual immorality; that each of you should learn to control his own body in a way that is holy and honourable, not in passionate lust like the heathen, who do not know God.'

1 Thessalonians 4:2–5

- The Bible forbids sexual immorality because it harms the body and the body is holy, the place where God's Spirit can be found.

Beliefs and teachings

'Flee from sexual immorality. All other sins a man commits are done outside his body; but he who sins sexually sins against his own body. Do you not know that your body is the temple of the Holy Spirit, who is in you and whom you received from God? You are not your own; you were bought at a price. So use your body for the glory of God.'

1 Corinthians 6:18–20

- The best possible love is a permanent and committed love, not a casual or temporary love.
- Some Christians argue that it is important to remain a virgin until you have found and married your true love. In America, some Christian teenagers started to wear purity (or chastity) rings declaring that they will not have sexual intercourse until they are married.

A   *A British student with her chastity ring*

Objectives

Explore Christian beliefs about chastity, sex outside marriage and adultery.

Key terms

Chastity: sexual purity. Not having sex before marriage.

Sex outside marriage: sex between people who are not married to each other. It may include adultery, sex before marriage or casual sex.

Discussion activities

1. Discuss these two views:

   'Sex is a personal thing. The Church should keep out of it.'

   'Christianity should mean more than what you do on a Sunday morning. It should affect every part of your life.'

2. Should Christians have sex before marriage?

3. Is chastity a virtue of the past?

Activity

1. Consider these three points of view. Identify the different points they make, make links between these views and the beliefs. What might each person say to the other to challenge them? Working in groups draft out some replies.

Beliefs and teachings

'You shall not commit adultery.'

Exodus 20:14

'I believe that when Genesis says that a man and woman come together, that means something really powerful, not a passing or temporary thing. I think God made human beings to make permanent commitments to one another so they can really rely on each other throughout their lives, facing all the ups and downs. Casual sex expresses little love. It's a momentary encounter action with little concern for the other person. If I live together with someone without getting married and times become difficult, how will I know that they will stay in there for me? Maybe they will just decide "time's up". I don't want to take that sort of risk with my life. I want a love that is commitment.'

(Person A)

'We should just accept that nowadays, sex is something that people get a lot of pleasure from. It should not be confused with marriage or commitment. If two people agree, then I don't see what's wrong with it. Doesn't God like pleasure? Anyway there are lots of worse ways of being evil. I don't think you should lie or go behind someone's back. If you are honest and consent to it, then there is no sin.'

(Person B)

'People who have sex before marriage are thinking about the now and not the future. What about the high numbers of unwanted pregnancies and abortions, the high level of sexually transmitted diseases? People today seem to find it really difficult to live together happily. Do we really think no-strings sex is going to solve all this human unhappiness?'

(Person C)

> 66 *The commitment is made in love for love … It is a profound sharing … It is a commitment through time. It embraces the future as well as the present. It intends and promises permanence.* 99
>
> *Church of England (1978)*

Study tip

The phrase 'sexual immorality' is in the Bible. Make sure you understand the different things that phrase might mean for Christians today.

Christian responses to adultery

In the Bible the Ten Commandments include 'Do not commit adultery'. Many Christians believe adultery is sinful because it undermines marriage causing suffering for the betrayed partner and threatens family life especially any children. People who have committed sexual sins should acknowledge their sin and change their life: Jesus said to a woman who had been involved in adultery, 'Go and sin no more' (John 8:11).

Extension activity

Look at the story of the woman caught committing adultery and Jesus' response to her (John 8:11). The story says little about the man committing adultery with her – what reasons might there be for this?

Activities

2 Consider the Christian arguments for chastity and against sex before marriage. Identify the strongest arguments of each and present a case from a Christian point of view.

3 Are there possible exceptions to Christian teaching on sex before marriage? Try to make the strongest exceptional case and compare your answer with a partner's. Evaluate the arguments and the evidence.

Summary

You should now be able to discuss Christian beliefs about chastity, sex outside marriage and adultery and be able to discuss them from different points of view.

3.4 Contraception

Contraception in Britain and the world

In contemporary British society the use of **contraception** to prevent pregnancy, either through the use of a contraceptive pill or a condom, is widespread. The availability of contraception is seen as one way in which couples can plan their families and women can lead working lives and more independent lives than in the past.

The planet's population will increase to 9 billion in the next few decades and some environmentalists argue it cannot sustain the current population. Birth control and contraception are suggested as ways of reducing this problem. The United Nations has promoted birth control as one way of reducing poverty in developing countries where overpopulation has stretched local resources.

Contraception has made casual sex more possible than in the past. It used to be considered very shameful to get pregnant if you weren't married. Since contraception helped change attitudes to casual sex in this country, the number of people with sexually transmitted diseases (STDs) has risen sharply. And not all casual sex involves contraception – Britain now has the highest rate of teenage pregnancy in Europe.

Different forms of contraception

Artificial contraception

These are forms of contraception which act as a barrier to new life – for example, the condom, which is a physical barrier preventing sperm from reaching the egg, and the contraceptive pill, a chemical barrier preventing the women from ovulating each month. Artificial forms of contraception, if used properly, are very reliable.

Emergency contraception

Emergency contraception, also known as the morning after pill, is a form of artificial contraception, taken up to three days after sex. It stops the production of an egg and/or stops eggs from sticking to the side of the womb. If the egg has been fertilised, this will stop it developing any further.

Natural family planning, or natural contraception

Natural family planning, or natural contraception, is the only form of contraception promoted by the Roman Catholic Church. It teaches that these are methods given by God to help a couple plan their family; they should not be used to completely prevent the possibility of new life at any time. One natural method is the rhythm method (getting to know the woman's menstrual cycle and the times when she cannot conceive, and making love in these times). Natural forms of contraception, if used properly, are suggested to be 85–98 per cent effective.

Objectives

Examine different forms of contraception and consider why they are used.

Consider moral questions raised by contraception and different Christian responses.

Key terms

Contraception: the artificial and chemical methods used to prevent pregnancy taking place.

Discussion activity

When couples make love, should they give themselves to each other openly and completely, or hold something back?

Extension activity

Research the internet for information about the issues of poverty, overpopulation and birth control.

The Bible and contraception

Artificial methods of contraception are not mentioned in the Bible. Some Christians think that Genesis 1:28, 'Be fruitful and increase in number', means God is against contraception. Others would say that contraception doesn't stop populations growing: it just helps families to not get too big for the parents to support. Also, Genesis and other parts of the Bible mention that sex is also about the two people coming together as one. It is not simply about reproduction.

Christian responses to contraception

Christian approval of artificial contraception

The Church of England Lambeth Conference of 1930 decided that it was morally acceptable for Christian to have sex for reasons other than having children and so approved the use of artificial contraception.

> 66 *The Conference agrees that other methods may be used, provided that this is done in the light of Christian principles.* 99
>
> *Lambeth Conference, 1930*

Many Christians believe that, while married Christians should try to have children, there is no requirement for them to try to have children every time they make love. Most Christian Churches see the use of contraception as entirely appropriate when used between a married couple. It shows a responsible attitude towards love-making and allows couples to plan their family.

Christian opposition to artificial contraception

The Roman Catholic Church is opposed to artificial contraception. It teaches that love-making is about making new life, as well as expressing love, and it should be open to both. The Roman Catholic Church teaches that any use of artificial contraception is a sin because the couple are not being open to new life when they make love and so are preventing God's plan.

Christian opposition to emergency contraception

Christians who believe that human life should be protected right from the point of conception are very concerned by emergency contraception. In the case of emergency contraception there is a possibility that the egg has been fertilised. Since the emergency contraception prevents the egg from developing, they would see it as causing the termination of a human life.

Activities

1 Why might a Christian couple believe they have a moral responsibility to control their family size?

2 Explain why the Roman Catholic Church is opposed to artificial contraception.

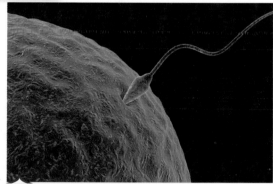

A *Being open to the possibility of new life is one of the purposes of love-making*

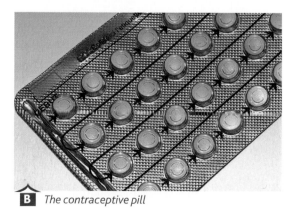

B *The contraceptive pill*

Summary

You should now be able to explain the different forms of contraception, suggest some moral questions raised and evaluate different Christian responses to contraception.

Discussion activity 👥👥👥

When the word drugs is used, what do you immediately think about? What do you think is included in that word, and what is excluded (for instance, would you include tobacco, alcohol, prescription medicines)?

Drugs have been used throughout history and in different ways by different cultures. Within some cultures drugs are believed to be a way of inducing states of mind that connect to the spiritual world. On the other hand, some drugs have caused significant damage to cultures. For instance in Arizona, alcohol misuse is a major cause of death and disability among native American people.

A person's use of a drug can start to control them and lead to physical and mental problems.

Objectives

Explore the different types of drugs and consider moral questions related to drugs.

Activity

1 Look at the effects of the drug types. Why do you think people take these drugs? Suggest reasons for each category.

■ Four types of drugs

There are four main groups of drugs. This book uses the word drug to refer to illegal drugs, medically prescribed drugs and alcohol and tobacco. In this table they are organised by their effect.

A *The four types of drugs*

Stimulants	Stimulants include caffeine and tobacco, as well as amphetamines, anabolic steroids, 'poppers', hallucinogenic amphetamines (including ecstasy), cocaine and crack. Stimulants affect the central nervous system, increasing brain activity. They tend to make people alert and less tired and lift the user's mood.
	High doses of most stimulants can lead to nervousness, anxiety and paranoid psychosis which is when a person loses touch with reality and becomes paranoid.
Depressants	Depressants include alcohol, benzodiazepines (such as Valium and Temazepam), and volatile sniffable substances such as solvents, glues and aerosols.
	Depressants reduce brain activity, relieve tension or anxiety and promote relaxation. They also reduce mental and physical functioning and self-control.
Analgesics	Analgesics are painkillers. They include heroin, opium, pethidine and codeine. Analgesics reduce sensitivity to emotional and physical pain, giving people a sense of warmth and contentment.
Hallucinogens	Hallucinogens include cannabis, LSD, 'magic' mushrooms and ecstasy. These heighten the appreciation of sensory experiences. Hallucinogens may distort people's perceptions, giving people hallucinations, feelings of insight and of being disconnected from the world around them or from themselves. They enhance a user's mood.

Source: Mind: www.mind.org.uk

■ Drugs, the law and society

Medically prescribed drugs

Sometimes there are stories in newspapers about overdoses caused by prescription drugs. Medicines such as pethidine and codeine are often prescribed for their pain-relieving capacity. They produce a sense of warmth and contentment which can become addictive. People develop a compulsive behaviour of having to keep taking them to reproduce the effects, rather than for any particular medical illness. People can become addicted to, or dependent on, prescribed drugs.

Extension activity

The National Drugs Helpline provides free help and advice 24 hours a day, seven days a week. Look at **www.talktofrank.com** to find out more about their work.

Illegal drugs

Illegal drugs are banned substances, and people can be charged with offences in possessing or dealing in them. In the UK these substances are defined under the Misuse of Drugs Act 1971 (modified in 2001). Offences under the Act include:

- possession of a controlled substance unlawfully
- possession of a controlled substance with intent to supply it
- supplying or offering to supply a controlled drug (even where no charge is made for the drug)
- allowing premises that one occupies or manages to be used unlawfully for the purpose of producing or supplying controlled drugs.

Drug trafficking (supply) attracts serious punishment, including life imprisonment, for the most dangerous drugs. Drugs are organised into different classifications according to their danger. Class A includes Ecstasy, LSD, heroin, cocaine, crack and magic mushrooms; Class B includes amphetamines and cannabis; and Class C includes tranquilisers.

Christian Churches are opposed to the use of illegal drugs:

> 66 *The use of drugs inflicts very grave damage on human health and life. Their use, except on strictly therapeutic grounds, is a grave offence. Clandestine production of and trafficking in drugs are scandalous practices. They constitute direct co-operation in evil, since they encourage people to practices gravely contrary to the moral law.* 99
>
> *Catechism 2291*

Socially accepted drugs: alcohol and tobacco

Alcohol and tobacco have traditionally been defined as socially accepted drugs. While there are laws that affect who may purchase alcohol and tobacco and where they may be consumed, they are not banned substances. Both alcohol and tobacco are socially much more acceptable than the other categories of drug. They are used for celebrations, socialising and sometimes (in the case of alcohol) in religious ceremonies.

Alcohol and tobacco are widely used, and can have devastatingly harmful effects. Far more harm is caused by tobacco and alcohol than illegal and prescription drugs, partly because they are widespread and easy to obtain.

Many Christians use alcohol in worship, basing this on Jesus' last supper and the practice of the early Church (1 Corinthians 11:24) while others oppose it (especially members of the Salvation Army, many Methodists and Pentecostal Christians).

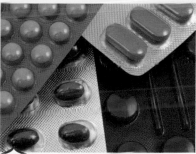

B   *Prescription drugs are often not thought of as drugs a person can become dependent on*

C   *Illegal drug use*

D   *Tobacco causes a lot of harm, but is not a controlled substance*

Activity

2   Consider what the different moral issues are that are related to drugs. Think about their effects and reasons why people might take them and make a list of the big moral issues.

Summary

You should now be able to explain the different kinds of drugs and suggest what moral questions are raised by drug-taking.

3.6 Drugs – an overview

A

Name of drug	Immediate effects	Long-term effects
Amphetamines	Make people feel alert, energetic and confident, with feelings of increased strength and mental ability. A single dose can last three or four hours. Afterwards a user feels exhausted for up to two days.	Frequent doses over time can make people delirious and cause panic, hallucinations and hostility. Long-term users may become psychologically dependent on the drug.
Anabolic steroids	Build up muscles. Are sometimes used as a training aid as they help the body develop quickly.	May cause aggression, reduce sex drive (in men) and lead to depression. Women may develop male sexual characteristics, including facial hair and a deeper voice.
Cocaine	Cocaine and its smokeable form, crack, have similar effects to amphetamines, but are both extreme and short-lived. Users tend to take them repeatedly.	Users are often nervous, excitable and paranoid. They may come to be uncomfortably restless, overexcited, and feel sick. Users may reach a state in which they believe that others are plotting against them.
Ecstasy or MDMA	Ecstasy heightens the sense of perception.	Taking it repeatedly in high doses can cause anxiety, panic, confusion and psychosis. As this is a relatively new drug, little is known about the effects of long-term use.
Solvents	Solvents, glues, gases and aerosols are typically used by teenagers for a short period. The user may feel dizzy, unreal, happy and less inhibited.	Repeated 'sniffing' can cause hangovers. Heavy users often have underlying family or personal problems. Sniffing directly from a pressurised container, such as an aerosol or butane canister, can freeze the airways and cause suffocation.
LSD	LSD creates a distorted experience of sounds, time and place. Users may have a heightened sense of self-awareness or feel disconnected from their body.	Users who are anxious or depressed may have an unpleasant reaction including dizziness, depression, disorientation or even psychotic episodes. People may have 'good' or 'bad' 'trips' at different times. Flashbacks are reported by some users, leaving them disorientated or anxious.
Cannabis	The effect of cannabis depends on a user's expectations and mood as well as the amount taken and the situation. Effects include a pleasurable state of relaxation, hilarity and enhanced sensory appreciation.	Low doses depress and high doses distort perceptions and confuse users. A depressed user may become very distressed if they take cannabis. The long-term health impact of cannabis is unproven but high doses cause panic attacks, confusion and paranoia. Dependent heavy users may seem apathetic, lacking energy and performing badly at school, university or work. Experience in taking this drug may lead to taking of other drugs.
Alcohol	Alcohol lowers inhibitions and heavy use can lead to a loss of orientation and control, and aggression.	Alcohol is a widely used depressant. Heavy users become tolerant and addicted. Addicts may use alcohol like heroin to 'escape' from problems. There are links between alcohol abuse and domestic violence. Long-term use can cause liver damage.
Tranquillisers	Regular drug users may take tranquillisers as an alternative to a usual drug. Tranquillisers relieve tension and anxiety, making users feel calm and relaxed. They do not affect alertness and clarity of thought and so GPs prescribe them for people who are depressed or suffering from anxiety.	Users may become dependent on them and need them to cope with ordinary life. Dependent users may feel severe anxiety and panic if the drugs aren't available.

Source: Mind: www.mind.org.uk

The politics of drugs

According to the UK Government Science Select Committee, the most harmful drugs are:

1 heroin
2 cocaine
3 barbiturates
4 street methadone
5 alcohol.

An RSA Commission on Illegal Drugs came to the conclusion that:

- 'More people are harmed by alcohol and tobacco currently than by illegal drugs.'
- 'More people are killed every year by sniffing glue than by snorting cocaine.'

Some legal drugs do much more harm than controlled substances. However, social acceptability makes tackling the issue of legal drugs difficult. There have been suggestions that some drugs, such as cannabis, should be left up to individuals to choose to use or not in the same way as tobacco and alcohol are left up to individual choice. Others argue this would allow an existing problem to get worse.

B *Some drugs are more socially acceptable than others*

Summary

You should now be able to explain some of the effects and dangers of different drugs. You should be able to discuss issues raised by their use.

Although the Bible does not refer to most drugs and their use, it does contain many references which Christians use to inform their responses to drugs. It also contains specific references to alcohol. Christian responses to all drugs are informed by views related to how they might harm the body and how they might affect the relationship with God and with others.

Alcohol, Christian worship and the Temperance Movement

Eucharistic wine

Many Churches use alcohol in the Eucharistic Holy Communion services because at the Last Supper Jesus shared the cup of wine:

> 66 *In the same way, after supper he took the cup, saying, 'This cup is the new covenant in my blood; do this, whenever you drink it, in remembrance of me.'* 99
>
> *1 Corinthians* 11:25

For instance, the Roman Catholic Church and Church of England use wine at the Eucharist, but some other Churches, including some Methodist and United Reform Churches, use non-alcoholic wine.

Temperance and abstention

However, Christians have also been associated with abstention from alcohol. Other biblical passages have warnings about alcohol:

> 66 *Therefore do not be foolish, but understand what the Lord's will is. Do not get drunk on wine, which leads to debauchery. Instead, be filled with the Spirit.* 99
>
> *Ephesians* 5:17–18

As early as 1832 the Primitive Methodist Church started teaching temperance – a movement to reduce the use of alcohol. There were divisions within the Wesleyan Churches but teetotalism (not drinking alcohol at all) was popular amongst some. The 1987 Methodist Report 'Through a Glass Darkly' invites all Methodists to 'make a personal commitment either to total abstinence or to responsible drinking'; and to 'give support wherever possible and by appropriate means to those who suffer directly or indirectly from alcohol misuse'.

The Assemblies of God encourage all Pentecostal Christians to abstain:

> 66 *[W]e urge all believers to avoid the Satanic tool of alcohol which destroys lives, damns souls and blights society.* 99
>
> *Assemblies of God, Pentecostal*

A *Wine is an integral part of some Christian rituals*

Members of The Salvation Army promise not to use alcohol and other intoxicants as a condition of full membership. Many other Christians might drink alcohol in moderation.

The body as a temple of the Holy Spirit

St Paul wrote that Christians should see their bodies as temples of the Holy Spirit and that the destruction of this body (temple) was wrong. Any kind of drug use which leads to harm to the human body is considered by many Christians to go against St Paul's teachings and be wrong. Christians are called to be filled with the spirit, not polluted by alcoholic spirits or other intoxicants.

Beliefs and teachings

'Do you not know that your body is a temple of the Holy Spirit, who is in you, whom you have received from God? You are not your own; you were bought at a price. Therefore honour God with your body.'

1 Corinthians 6:19–20

'Don't you know that you yourselves are God's temple and that God's Spirit lives in you? If anyone destroys God's temple, God will destroy him; for God's temple is sacred, and you are that temple.'

1 Corinthians 3:16–17

'Avoid every kind of evil.'

1 Thessalonians 5:22

Many Christians see people suffering from drug addiction and drug dependency as needing help.

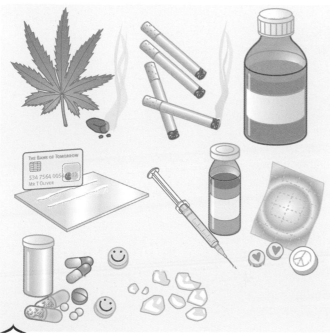

B *Different types of drugs*

Summary

You should now be able to explain different Christian responses to drug use.

Activity

Explain two different Christian responses to alcohol and give reasons for the different responses.

Extension activity

Do some research into the different ways in which alcohol causes harm to society. Consider drink driving, domestic violence, and street violence.

Study tip

Some Christians see socially accepted drugs in the same light as illegal drugs while others do not. Make sure you understand the differences in their responses.

What are the effects on those who take drugs, and on others?

There is a great deal of concern about the increasing use of illegal drugs, and their effects. There are immediate effects on the physical and mental health of the person taking drugs, but there are also damaging effects on the immediate and close family and wider society.

The New Testament states that people should 'love their neighbour' and also love their neighbour as themselves. Things that harm themselves and their neighbour are a problem for Christians.

> 66 *The Christian's faith teaches him to use all things, including his money, responsibly. He seeks to meet problems and stresses by following Christ's teaching of living by His power ... He loves his neighbour and therefore examines the probable effect of his behaviour, his habits and his example upon his neighbour.* 99
>
> *Statement by the Methodist Church, 1974*

▇ The effects on the individual

- Drug use can lead to dependency on the drug (be it legal or illegal). This may mean a person is psychologically and emotionally unable to live life without the drug. Here the value of life, the wellbeing of the person and their quality of life are diminished.
- Drug use can lead to physical addiction where the body reacts severely to the withdrawal of a drug and encourages the user to continue taking the drug.
- Harmful health effects: drugs can cause harmful side effects. Heavy alcohol and tobacco consumption can result in a whole range of health problems including liver disease, lung cancer and heart disease. Some drugs have long-term psychiatric effects and some can directly harm the human body if taken repeatedly over a long periods. Drugs can cause anxiety, depression, disrupted sleep and reduced wellbeing. Some drugs can have damaging effects even if only taken once.

> **Beliefs and teachings**
>
> 'The use of drugs inflicts very grave damage on human health and life.'
>
> *Catechism* 2291

▇ The effects on the family

Any drug-dependent addict is in danger of seeing their addiction as more important than those around them. As they become more and more dependent, they may turn to crime to finance the habit.

- Alcohol misuse can lead to drunken behaviour including violence. Partners may experience domestic violence and sexual assault because of the alcohol.
- Parents may neglect their children and their needs because the drive to spend money on their drugs is much greater than their feeling of responsibility for others.
- Addicts may steal from family members, including parents and children, to fund the drug habit.

- In the case of smoking, passive smoking means that those people around a smoker can risk the same health problems as the smoker themselves because they breathe the smoke in too.
- Pregnant women who smoke, drink in excess or take drugs can damage the health of their unborn baby.

◼ The effects on society

The cost of smoking for the UK

Research suggests:

- In the last 50 years smoking has caused the deaths of 6.3 million people in the UK.
- Smoking kills over 120,000 people in the UK a year – more than 13 people an hour.
- Treating illness and disease caused by smoking is estimated to cost the National Health Service up to £1.7 billion.

> 66 *On average, those who continue to smoke lose 10 years of life but stopping smoking at ages 60, 50, 40 or 30 gains 3, 6, 9 or the full 10 years of life expectancy. Of those who continue to smoke, half will be killed by their habit.* 99
>
> Sir Richard Peto, Professor of Medical Statistics and Epidemiology, Oxford University

The cost of alcohol abuse

The Alcohol Needs Assessment Research Report, published in November 2006, identified that:

- £217 million was spent in 2003–04 by the NHS to support alcohol treatment in England alone.
- About 1 in 16 of all hospital admissions are for alcohol-related causes.
- Since 1997 in England hospital admissions with alcohol-related causes have virtually doubled to over 250,000 cases.

Illegal drugs and crime

Research links drugs to crime but there are different suggestions about how the link works:

- Drug use causes crime. Perhaps as a result of the effects of the drug (a drug is consumed and the consumer then commits a crime because of the state they are in) or as a result of what is referred to as 'economic necessity' (illegal drugs are expensive, regular or dependent drug users typically have limited legal or financial resources to fund them, so they commit crime).
- Crime causes drug use. Funds from crime can be spent on various pleasurable pursuits, including drug use.
- Drug use and crime are 'reciprocal'. Sometimes drug use causes crime and sometimes crime causes drug use.
- Drug use and crime are both explained by a common cause. For example, it is part of a subculture, such as a gang behaviour, which encourages both.

Activities

1. Use the information on this page to construct a flow chart of causes and effects relating individual, family and society effects.
2. Which is the most damaging effect of drug use in your view? Give reasons for your answer.

Extension activity

Using the internet, newspapers or other sources, find examples of how drug taking causes harm.

A   *Why is addiction a problem for both an individual and for society?*

Summary

You should now be able to explain the different effects of drug use on people, the user and others, and consider the moral issues raised by those effects.

Drug behaviour and Christian action

Why do people start using illegal drugs?

For most people the first time they use drugs is because a friend offers it to them. People continue to use drugs because they find it enjoyable to do so. This might also be down to encouragement or pressure from friends, a sense of rebellion or just curiosity. It is suggested that as many as half of young people have experimented with drugs or solvents.

Different kinds of drug behaviour

The charity Mind divides drug behaviour into these categories:

A

Abstinence	Not taking a drug/drugs. It may have been tried and disliked.
Experimentation	Trying a drug out, perhaps on a number of occasions before making a decision about whether to carry on. Some drugs have little effect in the beginning (cannabis, for instance), others can have negative effects in the beginning (such as cigarettes). Most experimenters do not continue for long.
Casual, recreational and regular use	If an experimenter decides to continue using a drug, they may use it: ■ casually (when it is easily available) ■ recreationally (for particular occasions, such as alcohol when going out) ■ regularly (on most days). Drug users believe drugs enhance their lives without negative consequences.
Dependent, problem and chaotic use	People may slip into dependent, problem or chaotic use. It may be to do with them as a person, their situation, or the drugs they are using. Someone with serious anxieties or personal difficulties may use drugs in a problem way from the beginning. Some drugs make users become physically dependent (addicted) so that their body needs the drug to function normally. A person may become psychologically dependent on any drug for support. Users face unwanted, and sometimes harmful, physical, social, legal, financial or mental health consequences, as a result of their use. Chaotic drug use means the person isn't caring for themselves or others. Their life deteriorates as it becomes focused on getting hold of the drugs and taking them. Nothing else matters as much or at all, even their own health.

Extracted and simplified from www.mind.org

Helping people with addiction problems

For many Christians, because of their belief in love and forgiveness, drug addicts are not people to be ignored by society but helped and healed. Jesus spent time with some of the outcasts of his time and healed the sick. The following case study gives an example of how some Christians have responded to those who have become addicted to drugs.

Objectives

Investigate why people take legal and illegal drugs.

Discussion activity

1   Which of these do you think is drug use is most closely associated with in the beginning:

   a   a search for happiness or pleasure

   b   a search for belonging/ desire to belong to a group

   c   curiosity?

Activities

1   Using Table **A**, construct a list of reasons why a person may take legal and illegal drugs?

2   Which reasons do you think people should be most worried about?

Case study

In the 1960s and 1970s, two Christian couples – Doug and Barbara Henry and Bill and Joanie Yoder – met some young people who were addicted to drugs, and felt they had to do something to help them. Both opened their homes to many whom the world would normally shun, but soon found the work out-grew these houses.

In 1968 Doug and Barbara opened a rehabilitation home in Andover, followed by another in 1971 – these are known as the Coke Hole Centres. In 1977 Bill and Joanie opened a rehabilitation house for men at Yeldall Manor in Berkshire. Now, in 2001, these two charities are coming together to make a new one – 'Yeldall Bridges'.

The rehabilitation houses have grown and developed over the years and now house up to 46 men. These homes operate programmes of between six and eleven months for men whose addiction to drugs or alcohol has become very severe. These people, whose descent into addiction began with just a 'harmless' drink or spliff (of cannabis), got to the point where virtually nothing else mattered except the drink or drugs. Many lost jobs and families because of their addiction and, although they tried to stop, the withdrawal symptoms were so severe that their past efforts failed.

Source: www.request.org.uk/main/action/yeldall/yeldall01.htm

Activity

3 In what ways does this case study show Christian beliefs and attitudes?

B   *Most people are first offered drugs by a friend*

Extension activity

'Drug users are a waste of space, they bring harm on themselves, families and society.'

'People with addiction problems are sick and need help and care?'

'I think people use drugs as a way of blocking out things in life which make them sad. Life sometimes doesn't go your way and lots of people use drugs as a crutch to help them get through a crisis. What they need is spiritual help to finding meaning in their life.'

Consider these three views and write (or role play) a conversation between the three people. What might they say or try to discuss with each other? Try to think of a story that each might tell to support their point of view.

Study tip

Make sure you can give specific examples of the sorts of things Christians and Churches do to help people with addiction problems.

Summary

You should now be able to explain different reasons why people use legal and illegal drugs and how Christians might respond to drug addicts.

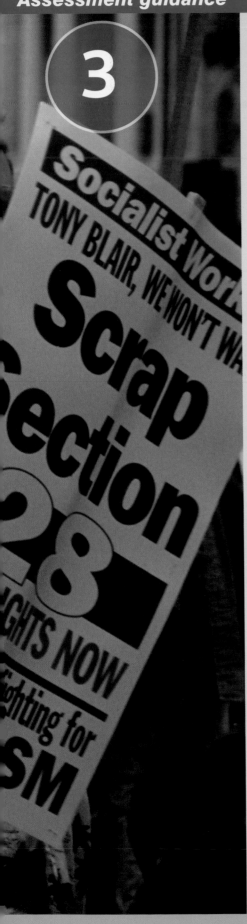

3

Personal responsibility – summary

For the examination you should now be able to:

✔ explain the terms sexuality, chastity, adultery, homosexuality, contraception, prescribed drugs, illegal drugs, socially acceptable drugs

✔ explain Christian beliefs and attitudes related to sexuality, chastity and sexual relationships outside marriage, including adultery

✔ explain different Christian beliefs and attitudes related to contraception

✔ outline the effects of prescribed drugs, illegal drugs, socially acceptable drugs

✔ give reasons why people take prescribed drugs, illegal drugs, socially acceptable drugs

✔ explain different Christian beliefs and attitudes related to drug taking and give examples of how they respond to addicts.

Sample answer

1 Write an answer to the following exam question.

'Explain why some Christians are opposed to homosexuality'.

(6 marks)

2 Read the following sample answer:

'The Bible says that a man and a woman come together. It does not say that two men or two women come together. Also St Paul says that homosexual sex is wrong. Many Christians believe the Bible is very important to what they believe and so they follow what it says and believe that homosexuality is wrong. Some Christians believe that homosexual people should not have sex but there is nothing wrong with their feelings. They should stay celibate.'

3 With a partner, discuss the sample answer. Do you think that there are other things that the student could have included in the answer?

4 What mark would you give this answer out of 6? Look at the mark scheme in the Introduction on page 7 (AO1). What are the reasons for the mark you have given?

Practice questions

1   Explain briefly what is meant by the term chastity. *(2 marks)*

2   Outline Christian beliefs about homosexuality. *(3 marks)*

3   Explain Christian attitudes to the use of contraception. *(4 marks)*

4   'Christians should not have sex before marriage.' Do you agree? Give reasons for
    your answer, showing that you have thought about more than one point of view.
    Refer to Christianity in your answer. *(6 marks)*

Study tip Remember when you are asked if you agree with a statement, you must show
what you think and the reasons why other people might not agree with you. If
your answer is one-sided you will only achieve a maximum of 4 marks. If you
make no religious comment then you will achieve no more than 3 marks.

4.1 Introduction to marriage

Discussion activity

'Marriage is three parts love and seven parts forgiveness of sins.' (Lao Tzu, 600 BC–531 CE)

'Marriage is not a noun; it's a verb. It isn't something you get. It's something you do. It's the way you love your partner every day.' (Barbara De Angelis)

'The goal in marriage is not to think alike, but to think together.' (Robert C. Dodds 1919–1989)

'More marriages might survive if the partners realised that sometimes the better comes after the worse.' (Doug Larson, English middle-distance runner who won gold medals at the 1924 Olympic Games in Paris, 1902–1981)

Consider these views on marriage. What are they trying to say? Do you agree? Give reasons for your views.

Objectives

Explore different views of marriage including your own and give reasons for them.

Key terms

Marriage: a legal union between a man and a woman.

A very brief history of marriage

Marriage has changed enormously in the last century. Before modern times it was influenced far more by economic and social necessity. It was almost impossible economically for a couple to split up. People were probably much more willing to put up with an unhappy situation, because they did not really have a choice.

The experience of a marriage based on a loving and equal relationship has grown recently. If people want to split up, they are financially able to do so. Women are now able to work and live independently.

Yes, I will marry the one on the end.

A *In the past, equality and love were not necessarily important parts of marriage*

Religious and civil marriage

Marriage is a situation that is recognised in law. This civil meaning affects how the government treats the couple, their property, children and inheritance. For marriages to be recognised in the UK there must be a registrar involved.

Marriage also has religious meanings. Christianity has a particular idea of 'Christian marriage' which is more than a legal arrangement but is a commitment to God and the Church, as well as the other person.

⚭ links

See pages 70–71 for more on Christian marriage.

Activity

1 What do you think is meant by the phrase 'Christian marriage'?

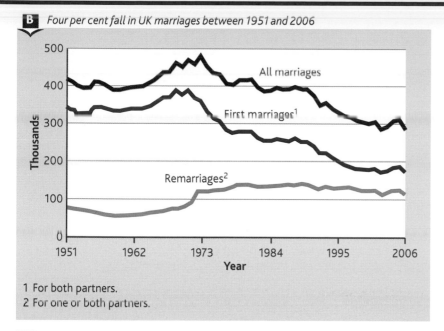

B　*Four per cent fall in UK marriages between 1951 and 2006*

1 For both partners.
2 For one or both partners.

■ Are people giving up on marriage?

In the present age some people seem less convinced that marriage is a good thing. In 2006 there were 236,980 weddings in England and Wales, the lowest number for almost a hundred years. Couples in Britain are getting married later than before. The average age for first marriages in England and Wales is 31 for men and 29 for women. Many people live together before getting married. In 2004 the UK passed a law which permitted same-sex couples to have what is called a civil partnership legally recognised. Some Christians believe these changes are threatening the importance of Christian marriage.

The values of marriage

Research suggest that not everyone has given up on marriage. Researchers asked what people thought getting married means. The most popular answer was 'committing yourself to being faithful to your partner'. Eighty-five per cent of people getting married say they intend to remain faithful. Over 60 per cent of the population see extramarital sex as always wrong. Divorce rates in the UK have fallen to the lowest number since 1985. In 2006, only 12 people per thousand married got divorced (although there were still 148,141 divorces in 2006).

> **66** *Mr and Mrs Lewis, a couple living in Margam, near Port Talbot, married in July 1938; and in 2008 they celebrated their 70th (platinum) anniversary. They were only parted for six years, when Mr Lewis served in the RAF during the Second World War.* **99**
>
> Source: BBC News

Summary

You should now be able to discuss different views about marriage and the basic difference between a civil and a Christian marriage.

Activities

2　What do you think it takes to spend all of your life with one person together in marriage?

3　Why do you think people are waiting longer to get married?

4　Do you think the recent changes 'threaten marriage'?

Extension activity

Your views about marriage may vary from those of others, because family experiences vary and often influence our attitudes to marriage. Gather views of marriage from people of different generations. You could ask people at school, teachers and other school workers, friends and family members. Don't ask direct questions about their experiences, but just their impression of marriage, their initial response to it.

What is the purpose of Christian marriage?

Marriage and love in the Bible

Christians believe that marriage is a gift from God. Genesis 2:18 and 2:4 say it is normal for a man and a woman to leave their parents and come together as one in loving companionship. They bring new life into the world and raise children in a loving family: 'Be fruitful and increase in number' (Genesis 1:28). Jesus repeats this when he says, 'But at the beginning of creation God made them male and female. For this reason a man will leave his father and mother and be united to his wife, and the two will become one flesh. So they are no longer two, but one.' (Mark 10:6–8). Marriage is about the love of the couple, the love of new life and the love of God.

Beliefs and teachings

Marriage provides the proper context for sexual relationships and the bringing up of children ... around which other relationships grow.

Church of England

Objectives

Examine biblical teachings on marriage and love.

Explore different ideas about the nature and purpose of marriage.

The nature of Christian marriage

B *Having children is one purpose of marriage*

A *Created for companionship*

What are the ideals of Christian marriage?

For most Christians, marriage is a lifelong, faithful love. The two people are expected to be completely faithful to one another. In marriage the couple promise to belong to one another and to continue to work at belonging to one another. The basis of Christian marriage is a love that supports and comforts one another. The love between man and woman should reflect the love of God. They should love each other 'as Christ loves the Church' (Ephesians 5:25). For many Christians marriage is the place for bringing up children.

Discussion activity

1 What do you first think of when you hear the word marriage?

a Write down all the words you associate with marriage.

b Swap your work with a partner and now try to construct sentences using each other's words.

Beliefs and teachings

[E]ach man should have his own wife, and each woman her own husband. The husband should fulfil his marital duty to his wife, and likewise the wife to her husband. The wife's body does not belong to her alone but also to her husband. In the same way, the husband's body does not belong to him alone but also to his wife.

1 Corinthians 7:2–4

If you choose to get married in church, there is an added dimension – the assurance that God cares about your relationship and that His resources and strength are available to help you. Including God in your marriage doesn't mean that you will avoid all the usual ups and downs, but you will know that you can look to God for help and guidance and that His love will sustain you. You will also have the support of the Christian Church family.

Your Marriage in the Church of England, Church of England

Love is as strong as death.

Song of Songs 8:6

C   *Christian marriage is lifelong*

Activity

1   Read the quotations about marriage and love. What messages do you hear in these words?

At the centre of Christian marriage is the love of one for another. It is a forgiving love, needed to overcome the challenges of daily life. It is a healing love, to restore and repair marriage. It is a joyful love, for delighting in each other and sharing in each other's happiness. It is not enough for one to care and love while the other just enjoys the benefits. Married life and love should be reciprocal.

Activities

2   Why do you think it is so important that couples learn to forgive one another?

3   In what ways can a couple bring healing to each other?

4   For Christians, how is sharing in each other's happiness close to Jesus' teaching of love?

5   What do you think the Bible means when it says that a husband's body is no longer his own but his wife's? And why might that be important?

Summary

You should now be able to discuss the purposes and nature of Christian marriage.

Extension activity

Read Genesis 1 and 2. What do you think it says about marriage?

Study tip

Makes sure you are clear on the different things that Christians believe about marriage. It is a loving and committed relationship in which new life might come.

> *Christians believe that marriage is a gift from God. In the marriage ceremony, a couple make a public declaration of lifelong commitment to love each other, come what may.*
>
> *Church of England*

■ Christian marriage preparation

In all Christian Churches the bride and groom are expected to have a responsible attitude to **marriage**. Because marriage is such a big undertaking most Christian churches expect couples to attend marriage preparation before they actually get married. This provides an opportunity for them to think through why they want to get married and understand the seriousness of their undertaking. Many Christian Churches expect the couple to have attended church for some weeks before the marriage.

A   *A church wedding*

■ Civil ceremony

A civil **marriage ceremony** is usually a short ceremony in a register office or approved building such as a hotel. There must be two witnesses who sign the register. The service includes the Declaratory Words: 'I do solemnly declare that I know not of any lawful impediment why I, [your full name], may not be joined in matrimony to [your partner's full name].' There are also the Contracting Words: 'I call upon these persons here present to witness that I, [your full name], do take thee, [your partner's full name], to be my lawful wedded wife [or husband].'

Objectives

Examine the conditions for marriage and explain why Christians believe they are important.

Suggest reasons why marriage needs preparation.

Identify the different parts of a marriage ceremony and explain what they mean and why they are important.

Key terms

Marriage: a legal union between a man and a woman.

Marriage ceremony: the ceremony in which a man and woman marry.

Activity

1   'Marriage preparation seems like a good idea. What about supporting people who ARE married with advice and support as well?' Explain why a Christian might argue that this is true. How might a Church community support the marriages within it?

B   *What do rings symbolise?*

A Church of England marriage ceremony

A religious ceremony has some differences from a civil ceremony.

Welcome
The minister or priest welcomes everyone and reads out what Christians believe about marriage.

Declarations
The couple make promises in front of God and to each other that they will love, comfort, honour and protect their partner as long as they both shall live.

Vows
The couple make their vows to one another: 'to have and to hold from this day forward, for better, for worse, for richer, for poorer, in sickness and in health, to love and to cherish, till death do us part.'

Traditional Church of England wedding vows

Exchange of rings
The couple exchange rings and say: 'With my body I honour you, all that I am I give to you, and all that I have I share with you, within the love of God, Father, Son and Holy Spirit.'

Traditional words for the exchange of rings

Proclamation
The priest tells the couple and everyone in the church that they are now husband and wife.

Prayers
Prayers are said for the couple. This may include prayers for the gift of children, and a blessing is given.

Readings
Appropriate readings are taken usually from the Bible, and there may be other poems or readings.

The minister gives a short talk or sermon about the importance of marriage to remind people about the meaning of Christian marriage, the nature of married love and the responsibilities of married people and of others to support the marriage.

Signing of the register
The bride and groom sign the register with two witnesses. This is a legal requirement and they receive their marriage certificate.

Quaker marriage ceremonies

Not all Christian weddings take this form. For instance a Quaker marriage ceremony is quite different. They believe that only God can join a couple in marriage and so a priest does not do this. A Quaker wedding may well take place in a Friends' Meeting House, as part of the usual service and may not include readings or hymns. Men and women will dress smartly. It will begin with a period of silence for some 10–15 minutes and be followed by the exchange of rings and declaration of vows. The certificate will be signed and there may be more silence. Other words may be said if the attending people feel moved to do so.

Summary

You should now be able to compare and contrast civil and religious marriage ceremonies and understand their meaning.

Activities

2 What distinctively religious elements can you see in the religious ceremonies which are not found in the civil ceremony?

3 Look at the religious ceremony and then, using pages 70–71, find teachings which relate to the different aspects of the service, and readings that might be appropriate for the Readings section. (You could make your own version of this table and add your new information into an extra column.)

Extension activity

Compare the two ceremonies listed here with a Catholic and a humanist wedding service. Use the internet and search for 'Catholic marriage rite' and 'humanist wedding' at a search engine. What similarities and differences can you observe?

Study tip

Be clear on the specifically religious parts of a Christian marriage ceremony so that you can explain the difference between Christian and civil weddings.

4.4 Alternatives to marriage

Cohabitation

Most couples in the UK live together before getting married, and some never get married. Some people want to have a trial period of living together to see if they get on with each other before deciding to get married. This is known as **cohabitation** or living together. Some people feel they should not have to commit to a lifelong relationship in a ceremony.

Christian responses to cohabitation

Christians offer different responses to cohabitation. Some are completely opposed to sex outside marriage so cohabitation is unacceptable. There are others who believe that marriage is the ideal state, but cohabiting long-term partnerships may provide a faithful and permanent relationship.

A

It is living in sin	Marriage is best but cohabiting couples should have their relationship protected
Many Churches see cohabitation as sinful because they teach that sex is only for marriage. The Greek Orthodox Church is opposed to any recognition of a relationship outside a Christian marriage. The Catholic Church also declares: 'The sexual act must take place exclusively within marriage. Outside of marriage it always constitutes a grave sin.' (*Catechism* 2390)	The Church of England Synod states that they: 'strongly reaffirm that marriage is central to the stability and health of human society and warrants a unique place in the law of this country; [and recognise] that there are issues of hardship and vulnerability for people whose relationships are not based on marriage, which need to be addressed by the creation of new legal rights'

Objectives

Explain different Christians' responses to cohabitation and civil partnerships.

Consider the moral and religious issues involved in those responses.

Key terms

Cohabitation: a couple living together and having a sexual relationship without being married to one another.

Civil partnership: legal registration and recognition of a same-sex partnership.

Discussion activities

1. Should a couple live together as a trial before getting married?

2. Is it right for gay and lesbian couples to have an opportunity to make legally recognised lifelong partnerships?

Activity

'Marriage is not for me. I have had enough of marriage breakdown in my family. I do love someone and I want to try and share my life with her forever but I can't commit to marriage. My parents tried that and it failed for them. I think my love and my girlfriend's love is enough for God.'

'I want to be able to stand up and declare my love for my husband, to him and to everyone else. If we are going to stick through the good times and the hard times, we need something to base it on. With the support of everyone at our wedding and after it, I think we have a better chance of staying the course.'

'I don't want to be living in sin. I couldn't bear knowing that what I am doing is going against God's law.'

1. Consider these three opinions. What reasons do they give to support their views? How might different Christians respond to each view?

■ Civil partnerships

In 2006 the UK Government passed a law that allowed gay and lesbian couples to have a civil union legally recognised. This gives gay and lesbian couples the same legal protections that married couples have regarding inheritance, pensions and also, in the case of medical emergency, being treated as a spouse.

B   *Does a civil partnership mean something different from a marriage?*

Christian responses to civil partnerships

Christian responses to **civil partnerships** are informed by beliefs about homosexuality, but there are differences.

Civil partnerships cannot have a Christian liturgy and should not be blessed

Clergy of the Church of England have been told not to provide services of blessing for those who register a civil partnership and there should not be a Christian liturgy for civil partnerships. However, there have been some clergy prepared to carry out such services.

A threat to Christian marriage

The Catholic Church does not recognise this as Christian marriage and considers this a threat to Christian marriage. Christian marriage is based on the biblical understanding of the natural order, that a marriage is between a man and a woman.

Civil partnerships are just as Christian as marriage

Some Christians argue: 'Gay people deserve the same right to marry that everybody else does. And God cares about our relationships the same way God cares about heterosexual relationships. We're making the same commitments to each other. We have the same responsibilities to each other, and we deserve the same rights and responsibilities under the law that everyone else has' (Harry Knox of the Human Rights Campaign).

> 66 *Promoting hatred and bigotry in the name of God is what destroys society, not the marriage of two loving people of the same gender.* 99
> *Letter to a newspaper discussing gay marriages*

Activity

2   What are the different Christian responses to same-sex marriage? Which of these do you think is the right response and why?

Extension activity

Working alone or in groups, draw up a table showing arguments for and arguments against cohabitation. Use the information from these pages to identify as many arguments as possible with reasons to support each argument.

Study tip

Make sure you are able to give Christian responses to cohabitation and civil partnerships.

Summary

You should now know and be able to discuss different Christian views on cohabitation and civil partnerships.

Marital breakdown

Marital breakdown can cause a great deal of distress for the couple and for their children, if the couple has them. It is the failure of something that everyone involved placed their hope in. It can lead to resentment, argument, upset and a profound sense of loss. The instability caused can be very difficult for children of all ages and can cause problems such as aggressive behaviour, a lack of emotional security, anxiety and depression.

What causes difficulties in marriage?

There are many different causes of tension in marriage. They include the following:

- Loss of the early romance of being in love: after marriage and the early time of 'being in love' it is important the couple become good friends as well. If not then unhappiness grows.
- Immaturity, excessive drinking and domestic violence all place tremendous pressure on a marriage.
- An inability to have children can cause suffering and tension between the couple.
- The death of a child leads to terrible pain which in turn may lead to difficulties between the couple.
- Having children is a lot of hard work and means the couple don't have as much time to spend on each other.
- Work and money difficulties bring about uncertainty and hardship, placing pressures on the relationship.
- Disappointment about love-making, especially if the couple give little attention to each other's feelings.
- Ill health – if a spouse or child becomes seriously ill, or disabled, this can be very testing for the marriage.
- Infidelity. Sometimes the attraction towards someone else can lure a person away from their husband or wife, especially if there are already other difficulties in the relationship.

Objectives

Explore different causes of marital breakdown.

Examine what can be done to prevent marital breakdown.

Key terms

Marital breakdown: when a husband and wife no longer get on with each other, leading to the end of the marriage by divorce or separation.

Activity

1 Look through the difficulties that couples may face in marriage: What sorts of things could a couple do to try to prevent these things from happening?

A *Communication problems can cause difficulties for couples*

■ What can be done to prevent marital breakdown?

Good marriage preparation

It is important for couples to be well prepared for the changes that will come about in marriage. Couples marrying in Christian Churches are expected to have some marriage preparation usually with the priest or minister. Good preparation can:

■ help a couple's understanding of their own unique relationship and the knowledge and skills needed to make relationships successful

■ encourage the couple to become aware of what they bring to their relationship, what helps and what hinders relationships

■ explore how relationships change and develop over time and understand ways in which difficulties may be faced together.

All marriages go through difficult times but many couples do not seek out help when they are having difficulties. They may feel embarrassed or may feel that their private life has nothing to do with others. In this situation the problems can get worse.

Good communication and reconciliation

Couples need to recognise that there is a problem and talk about it. Open and honest communication is essential. Christians must try to bring forgiveness and reconciliation back to marriages where problems have occurred and harm has been done.

External help

■ There are many organisations dedicated to supporting couples, such as Relate and Accord. They provide relationship counselling, help and advice.

■ Local churches often run special family days to support family life.

■ As with all difficulties in life, Christians are encouraged to pray for help to overcome them, and gain spiritual strength from prayer and worship.

> **66** *It's just so important to get help. You think you are the only one. You are so embarrassed to say anything. It seems easier to do and say nothing and just hope things will improve but there is help out there. Don't wait, don't allow things to get worse, get help.* **99**
>
> *Anon*

Extension activity

Find out more information about Relate or another marriage advice organisation. What sort of support do they offer?

Activities

2   Why could it be argued that good marriage preparation is essential?

3   Create an action plan for a local church to provide support for marriages. Look back at the list of difficulties that couples face – what sort of social and spiritual support could local Christians offer?

4   What advice do you think should be given to young people thinking of marrying about what they can do to help: (a) prevent difficulties in the first place; and (b) overcome difficulties?

Summary

You should now be able to explain different causes of marital breakdown and what can be done to prevent it.

Divorce in England and Wales

Divorce is a civil procedure when the marriage has irretrievably broken down. This includes instances of adultery, unreasonable behaviour or two years' separation or desertion. Couples are encouraged to seek mediation (advice and counselling) before proceeding.

A *In the UK there were 148,141 divorces in 2006.*

Christian views of divorce and remarriage

Christians have different views on divorce and **remarriage**, depending on their interpretation of the Bible and their beliefs.

Divorce and remarriage are both wrong

For some Christians divorce is wrong. The Roman Catholic Church teaches that civil divorce cannot dissolve a marriage between two baptised people. Any remarriage is therefore adultery. This comes from a particular Bible reading:

> Some Pharisees came and tested him by asking, 'Is it lawful for a man to divorce his wife?' 'What did Moses command you?' he replied. They said, 'Moses permitted a man to write a certificate of divorce and send her away.' 'It was because your hearts were hard that Moses wrote you this law,' Jesus replied. 'But at the beginning of creation God made them male and female. For this reason a man will leave his father and mother and be united to his wife, and the two will become one flesh. So they are no longer two, but one. Therefore what God has joined together, let man not separate.' When they were in the house again, the disciples asked Jesus about this. He answered, 'Anyone who divorces his wife and marries another woman commits adultery against her. And if she divorces her husband and marries another man, she commits adultery.'
>
> *Mark 10:2–12*

The Catholic Church does allow some marriages to be annulled. Annulment recognises a marriage was not properly valid at the time the vows were made perhaps because one or both were forced into the marriage, one or both never intended to have children or where one refuses to show any love or care for the other.

Divorce is possible, and in exceptional circumstances so is remarriage

Other Christians believe there may be exceptions. For instance the Church of England believes that although marriage is for life, sadly, some marriages do fail and that sometimes divorce is the lesser of two evils. In exceptional circumstances, the Church of England accepts that a divorced person may marry again, although not all priests are happy to do this and so special provisions are made for these situations.

Divorce and remarriage are recognised and accepted unless inappropriate

Some Christians take a more flexible view, both of divorce and of remarriage. For instance the Methodist Church is generally willing to marry people who have been divorced, while their previous spouse is still alive, as long as there are not major obvious reasons why it would be inappropriate to do so. People are human and they may make mistakes. Christians should reflect the forgiveness of God and offer people the opportunity of finding fulfilment and happiness in a second marriage. A Methodist minister may feel unwilling to marry a divorced person, in which case he or she will refer the couple to a minister who is willing to perform the ceremony.

B *Separation*

Activity

1 Compare the three different views on divorce and remarriage. What values and beliefs can you find in each view?

Extension activity

There are many Bible references which relate to divorce and remarriage. Look up the following in a Bible (there are online Bibles too) and relate them to the different views expressed in this page: Genesis 2:24, Malachi 2:16, Luke 16:18, Matthew 19:9, 1 Corinthians 7:10–11.

Activity

'As a Christian I think the Church should be forgiving and understanding of people who make mistakes in their married life. If things don't go to plan and the relationship breaks down, they should be allowed to start over and try again. The ideal is lifelong, but Christians fail in many ways. The Bible teaches that God forgives and the Church should show that by allowing people to try again.'

'Marriage is more than an agreement. It is a covenant. It is not just between the man and woman but with God as well. The Bible teaches that marriage is forever and that is the example that the Church should hold up so divorce and remarriage should not be accepted.'

2 Consider the two opinions. How are they linked to the Bible quotations? From which denominations of the Christian Church might these views come?

Study tip

Try to remember a reason for each of the different positions on divorce.

Summary

You should now be able to explain different Church teachings on divorce and remarriage and relate them to different understandings of the Bible.

4.7   The importance of family and the elderly

A *The family is important to Christians*

The importance of family life

Christians believe that families play a vital role in society. The wellbeing of the family is linked to the health and wellbeing of society at large. Families are the places to provide support, places of care for the young, the more vulnerable and the old. They are where children learn to share feelings and where the young can learn about life and faith.

Beliefs and teachings

'Here one learns endurance and the joy of work ... love, generous – even repeated – forgiveness, and above all divine worship in prayer and the offering of one's life.'

Catechism 1657

'The role of families is vitally important in caring for their members throughout the life cycle – in particular the nurturing of children, those with disabilities and the caring of older people, as well as giving opportunities for companionship, security, joy and fun.'

Church of England

Family pressures

Family life can face pressures from work, which diverts the attention of parents and, when it is not there, unemployment, which leads to money worries and anxiety. Marital difficulties, adultery and divorce can make family life difficult as well.

Some Christians will choose not to get married or have children, but to dedicate themselves to God in other ways. Nuns, monks and priests leave their immediate family in the service of God and the greater Christian family. Jesus taught, 'whoever does the will of God is my brother, and sister and mother' (Mark 3:35).

B *Family life*

Objectives

Explore the importance of family life and the elderly in Christian thought and belief.

Activities

1. What can a family provide for its members?
2. What sorts of pressures might families face that can make things difficult for them?
3. Why do many elderly people in the UK live alone?
4. What can the elderly contribute to a family and what responsibilities does the family have to the elderly?
5. How might Churches support the elderly?

■ The elderly in society

C What do you think this photo suggests about family relationships?

Beliefs and teachings

'Honour your father and your mother, so that you may live long in the land the LORD your God is giving you.'

Exodus 20:12

'Rise in the presence of the aged, show respect for the elderly and revere your God. I am the LORD.'

Leviticus 19:32

'Listen to your father, who gave you life, and do not despise your mother when she is old.'

Proverbs 23:22

Activities

6 What do these Bible teachings mean?

7 How might a Christian apply these teachings in their life?

The Bible emphasises respect for the elderly. Families should care both for the young and the elderly. The young need the wisdom and other gifts of the old. However, many older people live alone and are vulnerable.

D You should respect your elders

Extension activity

Use the internet to research support organisations for the elderly to get an understanding of the sorts of challenges they face in your society, and what can be done.

Study tip

When writing about parents, children or the elderly, try to show a depth of understanding by considering both what gifts they have to offer as well as the challenges they face. For instance, old people are not just a burden on society but a source of wisdom.

Summary

You should now be able to explain Christian views of the family and the importance of care for the young and the old.

4.8 The causes of prejudice and discrimination

1 Should we give different educational opportunities to girls and boys (for instance allowing boys to play football and girls to play netball, allowing girls to do Food Technology while boys to do Engineering)?

2 Do you think that people fear what they do not understand? Suggest reasons for your answer.

3 Should everyone have an equal opportunity to succeed and do well in life?

Objectives

Examine the causes and nature of prejudice and discrimination, and explain how prejudice is related to discrimination.

Key terms

Prejudice: unfairly judging someone before the facts are known. Holding biased opinions about an individual group.

Discrimination: to act against someone on the basis of sex, race, religion, etc. Discrimination is usually seen as wrong.

■ Prejudice and discrimination

Prejudice is an attitude of mind. It means unfairly judging someone before the facts are known. Common prejudices include the belief that black men are good at dancing and women are not capable of leadership jobs in society.

Discrimination means acting against someone because of their sex, race, religion, age, etc. Discrimination might include paying a woman less than a man for the same job, not giving a person a job because of their skin colour, not trusting someone because they are a different race from you. Discrimination is often against the law.

PREJUDICE CAN LEAD TO DISCRIMINATION

(attitude) ⟶ (action)

A

Prejudice and discrimination can be based on many different aspects of a person's identity, such as age (against youth or the elderly), religion and belief, disability, gender, race and sexual orientation (whether a person is homosexual or heterosexual).

Prejudice and discrimination reflect:

- inequality: not seeing another person as equal to you, or equal to 'your kind'
- fear: being nervous or uncomfortable with difference
- ignorance: a lack of knowledge and understanding about those who are different.

In societies which are plural and diverse, prejudice and discrimination can be particularly damaging.

B *Prejudice and discrimination*

■ Legislation on prejudice and discrimination in the UK

The Equality and Human Rights Commission is the government body responsible for working towards the elimination of discrimination, the reduction of inequality and the protection of human rights so that everyone has a fair chance to participate in society.

4 Is discrimination worse than prejudice?

C *Equality and discrimination rights*

Age	It is unlawful for your age to be the cause of less favourable treatment in your workplace or in vocational training.
Religion and belief	Your religion or belief, or those of somebody else, should not interfere with your right to be treated fairly at work, at school, in shops or while accessing public services such as health care and housing.
Disability	If you have a physical or mental impairment, you have specific rights that protect you against discrimination. Employers and service providers are obliged to make adjustments for you.
Gender	Women, men and transgender people should not be treated unfairly because of their gender, because they are married or because they are raising a family.
Race	Wherever you were born, wherever your parents came from, whatever the colour of your skin, you have a right to be treated fairly.
Sexual orientation	Whether you are gay, lesbian, bisexual or heterosexual should not put you at a disadvantage.

Source: Equality and Human Rights Commission

D *Equal rights*

■ Christian responses

Many Christians believe, that there is only one humankind and that a loving attitude be shown to all people, as all are loved by God and all are one in Christ. Prejudice and discrimination are often signs of sin.

E *You are all one in Christ Jesus*

Beliefs and teachings

'There is neither Jew nor Greek, slave nor free, male nor female, for you are all one in Christ Jesus.'

Galatians 3:28

'The Methodist Church is committed to eliminating discrimination and creating an environment where all people, regardless of gender, cultural or ethnic origin, disability, sexual orientation, age, religion or belief, are treated with dignity and respect.'

Methodist Church

Activities

1 How do biblical texts inform Church teachings on prejudice and discrimination?
2 How might these beliefs influence what a Christian does in practice?

Extension activity

Find a recent example of discrimination in the news which troubles or affects you in some way. Explain your feelings.

Summary

You should now be able to explain what is meant by prejudice and discrimination, the relevant UK legislation and Christian responses.

Study tip

Make sure you can clearly explain the difference between prejudice and discrimination.

Discussion activities 👥👥👥

A French journalist conducted an experiment in the Paris Metro. Actors, pretending to be a mugger and a victim, acted out muggings throughout the day at one of the busiest stations. For the most part people walked by doing nothing at all, even though the attacks were in plain view. The vast majority of people did nothing. They did not call the police and they did not intervene.

1   Why do you think so many people did nothing at all?

2   Do you think you would have done something?

Objectives

Explore the main features of the parable and suggest how Christians might interpret it.

Examine how Christians might act in response to the parable.

Key terms

Samaritans: a group of people in biblical times considered by some Jews to have abandoned the Jewish faith through marrying foreigners and taking on foreign religious beliefs.

■ Christian attitudes to the disadvantaged in society

It is easy to ignore the plight of others. Christian values identify the importance of addressing the needs of the poor and disadvantaged in society by standing up to injustice.

The parable of the good **Samaritan** is a story about what it means to be a follower of Christ. It is set on the road from Jerusalem to Jericho. There was great hatred between Jews and Samaritans. Samaritans had over the course of history intermarried with non-Jews and adopted many 'non-Jewish' religious practices, so they were viewed as having left the Jewish faith. Another point to note in the story is that priests had to take care not to come into contact with blood, as this would have made them impure and unable to perform priestly duties for a time.

∞ links

See the Beatitudes (Matthew 5:1–12)

Beliefs and teachings

'On one occasion an expert in the law stood up to test Jesus. "Teacher", he asked, "What must I do to inherit eternal life?" "What is written in the Law?" he replied. "How do you read it?" He answered: "Love the Lord your God with all your heart and with all your soul and with all your strength and with all your mind; and, Love your neighbour as yourself." "You have answered correctly," Jesus replied. "Do this and you will live." But he wanted to justify himself, so he asked Jesus, "And who is my neighbour?"

In reply Jesus said: "A man was going down from Jerusalem to Jericho, when he fell into the hands of robbers. They stripped him of his clothes, beat him and went away, leaving him half-dead. A priest happened to be going down the same road, and when he saw the man, he passed by on the other side. So too, a Levite, when he came to the place and saw him, passed by on the other side. But a Samaritan, as he travelled, came where the man was; and when he saw him, he took pity on him. He went to him and bandaged his wounds, pouring on oil and wine. Then he put the man on his own donkey, brought him to an inn and took care of him. The next day he took out two silver coins and gave them to the innkeeper. 'Look after him,' he said, 'and when I return, I will reimburse you for any extra expense you may have.'

Which of these three do you think was a neighbour to the man who fell into the hands of robbers?" The expert in the law replied, "The one who had mercy on him." Jesus told him, "Go and do likewise."'

Luke 10:25–37

Beliefs and teachings

'I tell you the truth, whatever you did for one of the least of these brothers of mine, you did for me.'

Matthew 25:40

Study tip

Make sure you know the parable and can apply it to different situations.

Activities

1. Who might the different people in the parable represent? Suggest two different possibilities for each person and give reasons for your suggestion.

2. In what ways might someone 'cross over to the other side of the road' today?

3. 'I never see anyone who has been mugged in the street. This parable hasn't got anything to say to me.' How do you think this Christian has failed to understand what the parable might be saying to him?

A *The good Samaritan?*

Interpreting the parable

There are many ways in which this parable may be interpreted and applied to Christian living. These include:

- Loving God and loving your neighbour are at the centre of what it means to be a Christian. Being a Christian demands action, not just beliefs.

- Christians have a duty to offer help to the disadvantaged – those who are rejected and ignored by society. The parable answers the question 'Who is my neighbour?' by suggesting that anyone in need is a 'neighbour'.

- Listeners would have expected the Samaritan to be shown in a bad light and the priest and Levite in a good light. Jesus deliberately reverses this.

- Christ stands with the poor and disadvantaged. He reaches out to and picks up the wounded, cares for them and offers them healing.

As a result of reading these teachings a Christian might:

- look at how their local church might be inclusive to disadvantaged Christians, for instance by installing a wheelchair ramp, or having a signed worship for deaf people

- make sure that Christians from all backgrounds are welcomed to church

- become involved in organisations dedicated to supporting members of society who are marginalised or discriminated against such as the elderly, disabled and those of minority ethnic groups

- look at how their local parish might be inclusive to marginalised members of society, for instance by installing a wheelchair ramp to improve access to church, by worshipping in different languages other than English so people who speak other languages can worship in their own tongue

- try to make sure that Christians from all cultural, racial and ethnic backgrounds are welcomed to Church and represented among the parish teams.

Activities

4. In what ways are the interpretations of the parable different?

5. How might a Christian apply the parable to the way in which they may see others?

6. Read the parable again. What meanings do you think it has for you today?

Summary

You should now be able to suggest how the parable of the good Samaritan challenges Christians to consider how they look upon others in society and what they should do about those in need.

■ Race and religion

Racism is prejudice and discrimination based on a person's **race**. Racism is a serious problem. There is also significant prejudice and discrimination on the basis of religion. Throughout the world there are examples of very serious racial and religious discrimination. In some countries people are not allowed to express their religious beliefs, or build places of worship. Christians in some countries live in fear of practising their faith.

The Stephen Lawrence case

Although UK law prohibits many acts of racism it continues to be a problem in society. Stephen Lawrence was a black British teenager from south-east London. He was stabbed to death while waiting for a bus on the evening of 22 April 1993. No one was convicted. After an inquiry into the investigation it was concluded that the Metropolitan Police Force was 'institutionally racist'.

Objectives

Consider examples of prejudice and discrimination in Britain.

Explore Christian responses to prejudice and discrimination.

Key terms

Race: a group of people with the same ethnic background.

Case study

Teenager faces 13 years for racist killing of Asian

Mr Rahman was attacked in the early hours of the morning as he returned from work to his council flat on a rundown estate. He suffered knife wounds to his back and front, but dragged himself home, where he was found on his hands and knees by his wife in the doorway. Noma Rahman has had extensive counselling since the murder, but the court heard yesterday that it had not helped her. Judge Hawkins said Mr Rahman 'was hard working and everyone liked him. His wife and children, aged four years and five months, were at home. He was a loving husband and father.' The Police said, 'The trigger point for this murder was that this man was Asian, in that it was a purely racial motive.' The teenager, along with three youths, called Shiblu Rahman a 'Paki' before the murder in April in Bow, East London. The Old Bailey heard that Mr Rahman, 34, had begged for his life during the attack and pleaded with them saying: 'Why me? What have I done to you?' The teenager who beat and stabbed an Asian chef to death on his doorstep was sentenced to life yesterday for the racially aggravated murder.'

Adapted from the article by Vikram Dodd, the Guardian, Saturday 15 December 2001

Girl wins religious bangle row

A teenager from South Wales has won her claim that she was discriminated against because she was not allowed to wear a religious bangle to school. Sarika Singh was told she was breaking the uniform's 'no jewellery' policy, and had been excluded from school for nine months. But the High Court agreed with her that it was an expression of her Sikh faith and that she was a victim of unlawful discrimination.'

BBC News Online, Tuesday, 29 July 2008

Discussion activities

1. How does racism affect society?

2. If you have a religious belief that means you feel you should wear a particular piece of clothing or item (such as hijab for Muslims, a turban for Sikh men, a cross for a Christian) should you be allowed to wear it in public, at work and in school?

A *Black and ethnic minority members of a Church*

■ Christian beliefs and responses

Most Christians believe that prejudice and discrimination on the basis of race or religion are completely opposed to the message of the Gospel because: 'you are all one in Christ Jesus' (Galatians 3:28)

> 66 *What does the colour of one's skin tell us that is of any significance about a person? Nothing, of course, absolutely nothing. It does not say whether that person is warm-hearted or kind, clever or witty, or whether that person is good.* 99
>
> *Archbishop Desmond Tutu*

> 66 *Racism is a sin. ... As Christian people we believe that with the coming of Jesus Christ a new relationship was initiated between people of different origins.* 99
>
> *Methodist Church 1978*

In 2008 the Archbishop of Canterbury accompanied the Chief Rabbi on a visit to Auschwitz to remember the Holocaust. Organisations such as the Council of Christians and Jews and other interfaith groups work together for greater understanding and against religious prejudice and discrimination.

Racial Justice Sunday is marked by Churches together in Britain and Ireland, an organisation for the different Churches. On the day some Churches recognise and celebrate cultural diversity in their own congregation.

> 66 *We must learn to live together as brothers, or we are going to perish together as fools.* 99
>
> *Martin Luther King, Jr*

Extension activity

Visit Human Rights Watch online (http://www.hrw.org) and download the latest *World Report*. In your PDF reader, conduct a key words search of 'religious' to scan through the various country reports. Find three examples of what you would consider serious religious discrimination and make notes on the details.

Activities

1   Explain the two quotes on the left using your own words and then relate them to the biblical teachings on pages 84–85.

2   How does racism harm society?

3   What does the Bible suggest about racism?

4   Using the information on this page, suggest three things a Christian might do as a result of their beliefs about racism and religious prejudice and discrimination.

Study tip

Make sure you can give specific examples of both the attitudes that Christians have and what they might do as a result of those attitudes.

Summary

You should now be able to explain Christian beliefs about racism and religious prejudice and discrimination, linking biblical texts to those beliefs.

Gender and disability

Prejudice and discrimination on grounds of gender or disability

Prejudice and discrimination on the basis of **gender** concerns the equality of men and women and the equal opportunities of men and women. Historically, almost all cultures and civilisations have been built around patriarchal communities (men having positions of power in public life and more legal protections). Today people continue to express sexist attitudes and treat people unfairly because of their gender.

A **disability** is when a person has a physical or mental condition that limits movement or activities. These can include cancer, diabetes, multiple sclerosis, heart conditions, hearing or sight impairments, a significant mobility difficulty, mental health conditions, or learning difficulties.

A *Examples of discrimination*

Gender	Disability
■ Men hold a greater proportion of senior positions of authority in business, law, medicine and education.	■ Physically disabled people do not have the same opportunities in work or education.
■ Women are paid less than men on average and in some cases less than men get in the same jobs.	■ People with mental illness face widespread discrimination from employers, even though one in six people suffers from mental illness at some point in their life.
■ Often when people hear 'doctor' they think 'man'. When they hear 'nurse' they think 'woman'. This reflects an expectation that the man will hold the more senior medical position.	■ There are increasing concerns that unborn babies detected as having disabilities may be aborted.
■ Some Churches allow women to be ministers or Bishops while others do not.	
■ Some Christians believe that men are the head of the family and that women should mainly stay at home and look after the children.	

Objectives

Explore ways in which people are discriminated against on the basis of gender and disability.

Examine how Christians respond to gender and disability discrimination.

Key terms

Gender: another word for a person's sex, i.e. male, female.

Disability: when a person has a mental or physical condition that limits movement or activities.

Activities

1. Should men and women be paid equal salaries for equal work?

2. Should disabled people just be treated with charity or should they be considered active and full members of society?

B *Women in the Church*

■ Christian beliefs and responses

Equality of person

Most Christian churches profess that men and women are equal:

> 66 *There is neither male nor female; for you are all one in Christ Jesus.* 99
> *Galatians* 3:28

They respond in different ways.

C   *Christian responses to discrimination*

Gender	Disability
■ Some Christians believe that equality must also include equality in gifts and callings. Many Protestant Churches admit women to leading roles as ministers and leaders in the Church. ■ Some Christians believe that, while women are equal, they have different gifts and callings from men and so should not be in leadership roles in the Church. ■ Some Christians believe that men are head of the household and that women should submit to their will. This is based in part on 1 Peter 3:1: 'Wives … be submissive to your husbands'; and Ephesians 5:22: 'Wives, submit to your husbands as to the Lord.'	■ Some Christians, like much of society, see people with disabilities as 'charity cases', while others see them as active members of the community. ■ Some Christians seek to support families with disabled children both materially and spiritually. ■ Some Christians believe the Churches should try to remove all barriers to full participation in the life of the Church – Bibles in Braille, celebrations with provision for the deaf, etc. ■ Some Churches teach children to sign hymns and songs of praise to help all feel included and make all aware of the different needs of others.

> 66 *To view people with disabilities as flawed and defective … is wrong for a church with Christlike compassion … Our faith and practice must include a compassionate hand extended to those with disabilities … They are people created in God's image, possessing dignity, value and purpose.* 99
> *Assemblies of God, Pentecostal*

D   *Does your local church ever offer a signed service for the deaf?*

■ Archbishop Desmond Tutu

Campaigning against racism and for reconciliation in South Africa

Desmond Tutu (born 7 October 1931) is a South African Church minister who rose to worldwide acclaim during the 1980s as an opponent of the apartheid government in South Africa. He was Anglican Archbishop of Cape Town, South Africa.

In South Africa at that time, the majority black population were not allowed to vote. They were housed in impoverished townships. Parents were split up for many months or years due to terrible work conditions. Black people were not allowed to use white facilities, and were excluded from many public services. Police beatings were common and black political opposition was met with assault, executions and torture. In 1976 a protest in Soweto against the compulsory use of Afrikaans, the language of the white minority, led to school children being shot and killed by police.

Desmond Tutu campaigned against injustice, rising in the Church and using his position to bring pressure for change through the international boycott of South African goods. He organised massive peaceful demonstrations and ultimately contributed to the release of Nelson Mandela and the end of the apartheid system.

He was awarded the Nobel Peace Prize in 1984 and the Gandhi Peace Prize in 2007. He went on to chair the Truth and Reconciliation Commission which contributed to the peaceful transition from the unjust situation of old to the new democratic South Africa.

Once, in 1993, before a crowd of 120,000 he said, 'We are the rainbow people of God. We are unstoppable. Nobody can stop us on our march to victory. No-one, no guns, nothing. Nothing will stop us, for we are moving to freedom. We are moving to freedom and nobody can stop us. For God is on our side.'

Objective

Explore examples of religious figures who have dedicated their lives to working against forms of prejudice and discrimination throughout the world.

Discussion activity

In a world where there is so much prejudice and discrimination, how should a Christian respond?

A Archbishop Desmond Tutu

B The effect of police brutality at the Soweto uprising

■ Jean Vanier and the L'Arche Community

Jean Vanier is the founder of L'Arche, an international organisation which builds communities where people with disabilities and those who care for them share life together. Jean Vanier felt called by God to set up a community in which disabled people and carers could recognise each others' unique gifts. Vanier believed that communities could change the world.

Vanier formed Faith and Light groups, made up of people with developmental disabilities, their family and friends. These groups meet regularly to discuss the hopes and difficulties they face in life and to pray together. Vanier believed that when confronted with human brokenness and weakness, people find a God whose love is without limitation.

There are now 130 L'Arche communities in 30 countries. They are found in different cultures with different religious and cultural settings but their work is based on living and working together and appreciating each others' value. Jean Vanier still lives in the first L'Arche community in France.

C   *Jean Vanier*

> 66 *Our community life is beautiful and intense, a source of life for everyone. People with a disability experience a real transformation and discover confidence in themselves; they discover their capacity to make choices, and also find a certain liberty and above all their dignity as human beings. The young and those less young, single and married, those with and without formal education, who commit on their part for a year or longer, they too experience a real transformation; they discover a place that gives meaning to their lives and their capacity to love and live out compassion and give life to others. The essence of our communities is this "living with". We are called, certainly, to serve with all our ability and to help those who are weaker to develop, but the foundation of this helping is found in friendship and the communion of hearts, which allows us all to grow.* 99

Jean Vanier, Il y a 40 ans, La Vie, 2005

Activity

1   Read the quote from Jean Vanier carefully. Explain what you feel are the most powerful messages in the quotation.

Activity

2   **a**   Explore how both Desmond Tutu and Jean Vanier have responded to their Christian beliefs and the needs of those who are marginalised and discriminated against in society.

   b   This could be through an interview. Think of what sorts of questions you might want to ask, and how they might answer. Think about the sources for their belief, the biblical teachings that you have studied in this chapter and how these may have influenced them.

Extension activity

Other Christians have worked against prejudice and discrimination. Find out more about Dr Martin Luther King, William Wilberforce and Anthony Benezet.

Study tip

Make sure you can give specific examples of how Christians are motivated by their beliefs to act against prejudice and discrimination.

Summary

You should now be able to discuss examples of religious figures who have dedicated their lives against prejudice and discrimination.

4

Social responsibility – summary

For the examination you should now be able to:

✔ explain the terms cohabitation, civil partnerships, marital breakdown, divorce, separation, remarriage

✔ describe and explain religious and civil marriage ceremonies

✔ outline the nature and purposes of Christian marriage and alternatives to marriage

✔ outline the reasons for marital breakdown and divorce and how these may be prevented

✔ explain different Christian beliefs about marriage, cohabitation, civil partnerships, marital breakdown, divorce and remarriage

✔ explain Christian beliefs about the importance of family and the elderly

✔ explain the terms prejudice, discrimination, racism, gender, disability

✔ outline the different kinds of race, gender, disability and religious prejudice and discrimination

✔ explain Christian beliefs and responses to different kinds of prejudice and discrimination, including the work of one well-known Christian.

Sample answer

1. Write an answer to the following exam question.
   'Explain Christian beliefs about racism.' *(6 marks)*

2. Read the following sample answer.

> 'Christians believe that racism is a sin. The Bible says that people should love one another and St Paul said that there is no Greek and there is no Jew. Because of this Christians believe that they should not be prejudiced and should not discriminate but should treat people equally. Everyone is loved by God and everyone was made by God.'

3. With a partner, discuss the sample answer. Do you think that there are other things that the student could have included in the answer?

4. What mark would you give this answer out of 6? Look at the mark scheme in the Introduction on page 7 (AO2). What are the reasons for the mark you have given?

Practice questions

1   What is mean by the word prejudice?   *(2 marks)*

2   Explain briefly what is meant by the term cohabitation.   *(2 marks)*

3   Explain Christian beliefs about marriage.   *(6 marks)*

4   'Christians should do more to help prevent marriages breaking down.' What do
    you think? Explain your opinion.   *(4 marks)*

5   'Remarriage is wrong, and against God's teachings.' Do you agree? Give reasons for
    your answer, showing that you have thought about more than one point of view. Refer
    to Christianity in your answer.   *(6 marks)*

Study tip   Remember when you are asked if you agree with a statement, you must show
what you think and the reasons why other people might hold different views.
If your answer is one-sided you will only achieve a maximum of 4 marks. If you
make no religious comment then you will achieve no more than 3 marks.

5 Global concerns

5.1 Christian beliefs about the world

Christian views on the world and the environment often begin with the creation story in Genesis. Genesis offers two different views which affect Christian attitudes towards the created world – that it has a special value and that Christians must live responsibly and be good **stewards** of creation.

The value of God's creation

In the account of creation in Genesis it states that 'God saw all that he had made, and it was very good' (Genesis 1:31). The created world is valuable and precious, and has a profound and important value. Many Christians believe that this is because the created world was made by God.

- The things created by God have value because the maker is God. He has said the world is good and human beings should take care not to damage or destroy things made by God.
- Some Christians also argue that the natural things of the world have a goodness in themselves because God has said so.
- Some Christians believe that the natural world was created for human beings to use responsibly. The food, natural resources, possible medicines and natural beauty are all things which enhance and enrich human life.

Activities

1. Are things valuable because they were made by God? How do Christians judge what is valuable?
2. Are things valuable because they have something good within them? What sorts of goodness do you think can be found in the natural world?
3. In what ways can it be argued that the environment enhances and enriches human life?

Objectives

Explore different Christian beliefs about the world and consider how these influence attitudes towards the environment.

Key terms

Stewardship: the belief that believers have a duty to look after the environment on behalf of God.

Discussion activity

'How many are your works, O LORD. In wisdom you made them all; the earth is full of your creatures. There is the sea, vast and spacious, teeming with creatures beyond number – living things both large and small. … When you send your Spirit, they are created, and you renew the face of the Earth. (Psalms 104:24–25, 30)

How might this quotation inspire Christian attitudes and actions in the world?

Stewardship and responsibility

Beliefs and teachings

Then God said, 'Let us make man in our image, in our likeness, and let them rule over the fish of the sea and the birds of the air, over the livestock, over all the earth, and over all the creatures that move along the ground.'

Genesis 1:26

Many Christians believe they should be stewards of the world. In other words Christians think that as human beings, created by God, they have a responsibility to look after and care for the environment. 'The earth is the LORD's, and everything in it, the world, and all who live in it' (Psalms 24:1). Christians are merely tenants on Earth. They do not own it.

Being a good steward might involve:

- preserving the environment for the people who are young now or are to be born in the future (loving the neighbours of the future)
- sharing the natural resources of the world fairly among people, rather than hoarding them for the rich few
- using the resources of the world in a way which is sustainable, and remembering that they were made by God
- joining groups which campaigning for or protect the environment.

A   *Many Christians believe that all of creation is a gift from God which must be cared for responsibly*

Creation in God's plan

The Bible suggests that God has made his covenant with the whole of creation, not just humanity and he is therefore interested in the whole world. Christians take from this the belief that God wishes to redeem the whole of the world, not just humanity. 'I now establish my covenant with you and with your descendants after you and with every living creature that was with you' (Genesis 9:8). And the created world is called to worship him and should not be destroyed:

> 66 *You will go out in joy and be led forth in peace; the mountains and hills will burst into song before you, and all the trees of the field will clap their hands … This will be for the LORD's renown, for an everlasting sign, which will not be destroyed.* 99

Isaiah 55:12–13

Discussion activity

'People of Earth ... This is Prostetnic Vogon Jeltz of the Galactic Hyperspace Planning Council,' the voice continued. 'As you will no doubt be aware, the plans for development of the outlying regions of the Galaxy require the building of a hyperspatial express route through your star system, and regrettably your planet is one of those scheduled for demolition. The process will take slightly less than two of your Earth minutes. Thank you.'

(from *The Hitchhikers Guide to the Galaxy*, by Douglas Adams)

Is there a more important priority for any human being than the survival of the planet and the life systems it offers?

Objectives

Investigate different environmental problems caused by climate change.

Begin to consider possible Christian responses to them.

Key terms

Climate change: changes to the climate, believed by some scientists to be irreparably damaging, that have been caused by human lifestyles.

What is climate change?

Climate change refers to the long-term change in the 'average weather' including the increase in average temperature, precipitation (rain and snowfall), and wind patterns. These changes can be caused by processes on Earth and external forces such as variations in sunlight intensity. A significant factor in recent climate change is human activity.

The increasing temperatures and increasing wind activity on Earth are leading to the melting of the polar ice caps and a rise in sea levels, together with more damaging storms and droughts. The evidence suggests that to continue to live as if nothing has changed will be a disaster for human civilisation.

The bad news

> " *Warming of the climate system is unequivocal, as is now evident from observation of increases in global average air and ocean temperatures, widespread melting of snow and ice, and rising global average sea level ... [M]any natural systems are being affected by regional climate change.* "
>
> Intergovernmental Panel on Climate Change, 2007, pp1–2

A   Temperatures are rising due to climate change

For 50 years or so, many simply did not believe that climate change was happening or thought that, if it was, it was nothing to worry about. Various alternative explanations were given for signs of global warming and these are still put forward sometimes. Occasionally these explanations still reappear in the newspapers.

However, virtually all scientists believe, and virtually all relevant research now shows, that the climate of the planet is changing and that human activity is the main reason for it. In other words, the burning of fossil fuels and production of chemical gases, alongside the destruction of natural habitats, has caused the increase in greenhouse gases in the atmosphere. These gases are involved in a process that raises global temperatures which, in turn, is driving climate change.

Activities

1 What is climate change?
2 What is the probable cause of climate change?
3 What are the effects of climate change?

B *The York floods. This is the kind of thing which is more likely to happen as a result of climate change*

C *The polar ice shelf has melted so much that ordinary ships can now sail through the north-west passage for the first time in human history*

The worse news

According to scientist James Lovelock, even if pollution and deforestation stopped here and now it would take the Earth more than a thousand years to recover from the damage we have done. Climate change is inevitable. It is already happening. It is not so much a case of stopping it happening as preventing it from getting much worse. James Lovelock thinks we need to learn how to live all over again. The way we have learned to live over the last 200 hundred years is not working.

The effects of climate change on human life

The consequences of climate change are serious for agriculture, forestry, ecosystems, water resources, human health, industry, settlement and society.

- Crop yields will be reduced.
- Deaths among the elderly and the sick will increase due to hotter days.
- Those without appropriate housing will have a reduction in the quality of life.
- There will be water shortages, more flooding and more wildfires.
- Poorer parts of the world will be hit earlier and harder by the effects of climate change. Richer countries can better protect themselves against the changes although there is no immunity – they will be affected.

Case study

Tuvalu

'Our island is sinking together with our hearts,' wrote Silafaga Lalua in *Tuvalu News*. Tuvalu is a small, low-lying island. The whole island is no higher than five metres above sea level. Now when the sea storms come the whole island is flooded. Climate change is leading to higher sea levels and more storms and Tuvalu is likely to become uninhabitable if temperatures keep rising. For the people of Tuvalu, climate change may lead to the loss of their world, in our lifetime.

Study tip

Make sure you can clearly state what several of the effects of climate change will be.

Extension activity

Find out more about Tuvalu and other parts of the world facing the consequences of climate change right now.

Activities

4 If humanity was arrested for crimes against the Earth, what would the arrest warrant say? What would the charges be?

5 What do you think a Christian response to Silafaga Lalua's predicament should be?

Summary

You should now be able to explain what is meant by climate change, and what are thought to be the causes and the effects of climate change.

5.5   National and international responses

■ National responses

The Stern Report

In July 2005 the economist Lord Stern started a review of the economics of climate change. The *Stern Review on the Economics of Climate Change*, published in 2006, is the most widely known and discussed report of its kind. It concluded that:

- climate change was real
- human activity was contributing to it
- the world should spend one per cent of global gross domestic product (GDP) to avoid the worst effects of climate change
- if the world fails to do this then global GDP will fall by up to 20 per cent; this would cause dramatic world economic hardship.

UK Government policies

The UK Government is working to reduce carbon emissions in many areas, for example:

- finding non-carbon-producing alternatives for electricity generation including renewable and nuclear forms of power generation
- increasing regulations on buildings so that, for example, new houses must have loft and cavity wall insulation
- supporting the development of new, greener car fuels
- encouraging energy conservation and recycling.

■ International responses – Earth summits

1992 The Earth summit in Rio de Janeiro

This United Nations conference tried to rethink economic development and find ways to halt the destruction of irreplaceable natural resources and pollution of the planet.

1997 Kyoto Protocol

The Kyoto Protocol is an international Framework Convention on Climate Change which aims to reduce greenhouse gases by 5 per cent in an effort to prevent human-caused climate change reaching dangerous levels. The Protocol was adopted for use on 11 December 1997 and it came into force in 2005. By 2008, 182 states had signed the protocol. The goal is to lower overall emissions of the main greenhouse gases.

Some countries, such as Germany and the UK, have reduced their emissions, but many countries have increased their emissions, and these include three of the largest countries in the world, who have not signed the agreement: USA, China and India. Some claim that without the largest countries in the world agreeing to reduce their emissions, little anyone else does will help.

Objectives

Investigate national and international responses to environmental problems.

Begin to consider possible Christian responses to them.

Key terms

Earth summits: meetings of international leaders aimed at reaching an agreement that will reduce environmental pollution and climate change.

Discussion activity

The environment is in a bad state. Who should be responsible for making the changes we need to improve the situation: you as an individual; your community (home/school) around you; the government; the international community?

Study tip

Make sure you can give specific examples of national and international responses.

Renewable energy and the European Union 2020 targets

The European Union has committed to reducing its overall carbon emissions to at least 20 per cent below 1990 levels by 2020. It has also set itself the target of having 20 per cent of energy from renewable sources by 2020. This would mean reducing the polluting energy sources such as coal-fired power stations. Renewable energy sources are those which reduce carbon emissions and include:

- wind farms
- solar power
- power stations which do not release greenhouse gases.

At present these are ambitious targets but some countries have succeeded. Twenty per cent of Denmark's energy comes from wind farms, for example.

A *Renewable energy – wind farms*

Christian attitudes to Earth summits

After the 1992 **Earth summit** the Church of England produced its own report linking the findings to Christian faith and encouraging Church communities to respond.

Christian leaders have supported the messages coming out of the Earth summits and have encouraged ordinary people to respond. For example, the Bishop of Liverpool, James Jones, and the Bishop of London, Dr Richard Chartres, called for a cut in personal carbon use for each of the 40 days of Lent in 2008. This will

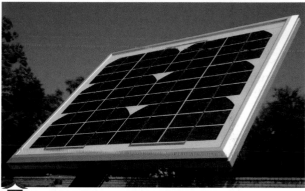

B *Renewable energy – solar power*

include not accepting new plastic bags, giving the dishwasher a day off, insulating the hot water tank and checking the house for draughts with a ribbon and buying draught excluders.

Pope Benedict has had 2,700 solar panels placed on the roof at the Vatican to heat a hall inside and has criticised the 'unbalanced use of energy in the world'.

Many Christians have become involved in ecological 'green' Christian organisations and networks which work to improve the environmental situation.

Activities

1. Give two examples of responses to environmental problems, one national and one international. Explain what they seek to do.
2. What role do you think Christian Churches should take in trying to tackle climate change and its consequences?

Extension activity

REEP, the Religious Education and Environment Project, was set up in 1994 to encourage the study of environmental issues in the context of religious insights. Find out more about it at **www.reep.org**.

Summary

You should now be able to describe national and international responses to the environmental problems, and Christian attitudes to these responses.

5.7 Christian beliefs about respect for each other

The mission of love: justice and respect for all

Beliefs and teachings

If anyone has material possessions and sees his brother in need but has no pity on him, how can the love of God be in him? Dear children, let us not love with words or tongue but with actions and in truth.

1 John 3:17–18

For Christians, if someone does not have compassion for a fellow human being how can the love of God be in him or her?

According to the Gospel,

- The poor are blessed and the kingdom of heaven is theirs (Luke 6:20).
- The poor are waiting for justice (Luke 1:17).

Christians believe they have a duty to attend to the demands of **justice** and peace. They must show respect for people, since for God loves the world, the whole human family.

Why do people matter?

'The glory of God is a person fully alive' (St Irenaeus). Many Christians believe that every single human being has dignity and should be respected. The human person is a sacred, unique being, created by God and in his image (Genesis), to be treated with love: 'love your neighbour'.

A single human family

The Bible commands Christians to love their neighbour as themselves. Loving your neighbour includes actively caring for those in need. Jesus told a story to explain this.

The parable of sheep and the goats

Beliefs and teachings

When the Son of Man comes in his glory, and all the angels with him, he will sit on his throne in heavenly glory. All the nations will be gathered before him, and he will separate the people one from another as a shepherd separates the sheep from the goats. He will put the sheep on his right and the goats on his left. Then the King will say to those on his right, 'Come, you who are blessed by my Father; take your inheritance, the kingdom prepared for you since the creation of the world. For I was hungry and you gave me something to eat, I was thirsty and you gave me something to drink, I was a stranger and you invited me in, I needed clothes and you clothed me, I was sick and you looked after me, I was in prison and you came to visit me.'

Then the righteous will answer him, 'Lord, when did we see you hungry and feed you, or thirsty and give you something to drink? When did we see

A *In the image and likeness of God*

you a stranger and invite you in, or needing clothes and clothe you? When did we see you sick or in prison and go to visit you?'

The King will reply, 'I tell you the truth, whatever you did for one of the least of these brothers of mine, you did for me.' Then he will say to those on his left, 'Depart from me, you who are cursed, into the eternal fire prepared for the devil and his angels. For I was hungry and you gave me nothing to eat, I was thirsty and you gave me nothing to drink, I was a stranger and you did not invite me in, I needed clothes and you did not clothe me, I was sick and in prison and you did not look after me.'

They also will answer, 'Lord, when did we see you hungry or thirsty or a stranger or needing clothes or sick or in prison, and did not help you?'

He will reply, 'I tell you the truth, whatever you did not do for one of the least of these, you did not do for me.' Then they will go away to eternal punishment, but the righteous to eternal life.

Matthew 25:31–46

Matthew 25:31–46 is a powerful text, and much Christian teaching about action is based on it:

- Christianity is a religion where love for God is shown through deeds of practical loving kindness – this is an essential part of Christian faith.
- Love of neighbour is essential to what it means to be Christian, not an afterthought or optional extra.
- Love for Jesus is expressed through love and service to the needy.
- Human beings have a moral responsibility to do their duty for those in need.
- God takes human actions really seriously.

The works of mercy: actions of love

The text also identifies some particular ways in which Christians should demonstrate practical loving kindness. These include:

- visiting and looking after the sick and those in prison
- providing for those who are hungry and thirsty
- caring for strangers
- clothing and respecting those who have lost everything, who are stripped of dignity ('naked').

Christians are bound then to care for those in need out of love for God, obedience to Jesus and respect for human beings.

B *One human family*

Summary

You should now be able to explain different reasons why Christians believe that human beings need respect, especially those who are poor. They should respect all human beings and help those in need.

What are the causes of world poverty?

Man-made or environmental?

Traditionally people have thought that usually poverty is caused by unfortunate environmental influences such as natural disasters. Increasingly, however, poverty is the result of human activity. Look at the table below for some examples of the causes of **world poverty**.

A *Causes and impact of world poverty*

Cause	Impact
Environmental problems	Frequent natural disasters, such as droughts, destroy crops which mean whole communities are seriously weakened. Poor countries do not have the resources to overcome such disasters so families go unfed, workers become weaker and more prone to disease and less fit to work when conditions change. Increasingly, natural disasters may be the result of man-made pollution of the environment.
Healthcare	The lack of basic healthcare means child mortality is high, women are more likely to die in childbirth, preventable illnesses make people seriously ill, and people die unnecessarily. This makes it very difficult for families and communities to develop economically.
Conflict	Warfare and civil strife within and between countries take resources and workers away into conflict, while services such as health and education, and agriculture suffer. Conflict often drives people from their homes and destroys their way of earning a living leaving them unable to live safe and productive lives.
Bad government	Corruption and mismanagement waste resources and lead to bad decisions by leaders. Relatively stable countries have been brought to economic collapse by corrupt rulers.
HIV/Aids	In some countries huge numbers of people suffer from HIV and Aids. Often the group affected are younger adults, an important part of the workforce. They die young or are seriously weakened, meaning the country cannot develop.
Debt	Poorer countries have had to borrow large sums of money from rich countries in the past and now have to pay back the loans rather than spend money on their own people.
Trade barriers	Unfair trade rules benefit richer countries. They mean that many very poor countries are prevented from selling their produce to richer countries, or forced to compete against rich countries which use money from taxes to make goods cheaper.
Greed in more economically developed countries	The richer, more powerful countries are in a position to use their power and influence to take and consume far more of the wealth of the world than is fair, leaving others with less to share between them. Almost everyone who ever reads this book will be far richer than the majority of the people of the world.

Objectives

Explore and understand the different causes of poverty and the poverty cycle with reference to an example.

Key terms

World poverty: the idea that the majority of the world's population actually live in conditions of extreme need or hardship.

Discussion activity

Do you think poverty is an unfortunate accident or result of human action?

Activity

1 Suggest how Christians might respond to each of these causes.

The poverty cycle

Poverty can lead to a cycle of decline (the poverty cycle). For instance, if Aids/HIV has caused illness and death of the young adult workers, then:

- the older generation of grandparents are left to look after the children and work; so
- it is difficult to do both, so not enough wealth is made from working to feed the family; which leads to
- hunger and poorer health, which in turn means the person is less able to care for the children and work; which in turn
- leads to even less money to buy food.

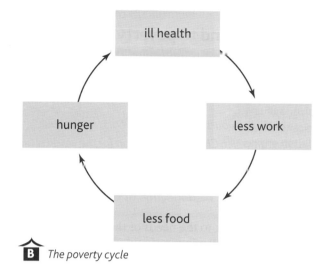

B *The poverty cycle*

Poor government

Zimbabwe is in the southern part of Africa. The country has been an independent state for many years with valuable resources and productive farms. In 2000 the Government introduced a land reform policy of taking farms from white owners and giving them to black people (often to supporters of the Government). Many farms were looted and fell into disuse. Zimbabwe now suffers from hyperinflation which means the money workers are paid quickly becomes worthless. Many people currently struggle to find enough food to feed themselves. Huge numbers of people have abandoned their homes and left the country in search of security and help. Zimbabwe was a productive country but poor government has caused its economy to collapse.

Case study

Extension activity

Use charity websites to find other actual examples of the causes of poverty.

Activities

2 Design a diagram or picture which illustrates the different causes of poverty.

3 Examine the case study and devise a flow diagram to show the stages of decline.

Study tip

Make sure you can explain human causes, as well as natural causes, of poverty.

Summary

You should now be able to explain the different causes of poverty and the nature of the poverty cycle.

Faith in action

Four Christian voluntary **aid** agencies dedicated to supporting the poorest and most disadvantaged, marginalised people throughout the world are Christian Aid, Tearfund, **CAFOD** and Trócaire. Their activities include:

- educational and awareness campaigns
- emergency relief (short-term aid)
- development projects (**long-term aid**)
- campaigning to to promote justice.

> 66 *Tearfund is a Christian relief and development agency working with a global network of local churches to help eradicate poverty. Our ten-year vision is to see 50 million people released from material and spiritual poverty through a worldwide network of 100,000 local churches.* 99
>
> *Tearfund*

A *Do we live in a material world?*   **B** *Christain Aid*

> 66 *Christain Aid works with some of the world's poorest people, of all faiths and none, to tackle the causes and consequences of poverty and injustice and to campaign for change.*
>
> *We work in around 50 countries with more than 650 local organisations, where there is great need.*
>
> *Our essential purpose is to expose the scandal of poverty, to help in practical ways to root it out from the world, and to challenge and change the systems that favour the rich and powerful over the poor and marginalised.* 99
>
> *Christian Aid*

> 66 *CAFOD believes that all human beings have a right to dignity and respect, and that the world's resources are a gift to be shared equally by all men and women, whatever their race, nationality or religion … CAFOD works for justice with partners in more than 50 countries to provide long-term development programmes and humanitarian relief.* 99
>
> *CAFOD*

C *CAFOD*

> 66 *Trócaire is working for a just world where people's dignity is ensured, the rights of individuals are respected and where basic needs are met ... to support long-term development projects overseas and to provide relief during emergencies.* 99
>
> Trócaire

TRÓCAIRE
Working for a Just World
D   *Trócaire*

Raising awareness

Charities and aid agencies inspired by Christianity work to educate people in richer countries about the situation for people in poorer countries using leaflets, posters, books, videos, the internet and working through the Churches. Different themes and projects are selected from year to year, responding to new and ongoing emergencies. Education teams work with school, church and other community groups raising awareness and encouraging fundraising activities.

They also work for justice in the world, defending the rights of the poor and marginalised, throwing light on injustice and disadvantage. Examples of this work include providing help for people living with HIV/Aids and also helping women, who are often disadvantaged and discriminated against, often not having access to education and jobs.

Emergency aid (short-term aid)

Through local organisations throughout the world, organisations such as Christian Aid and CAFOD respond very quickly to sudden emergencies and disasters – for example, helping those affected provide food or shelter for themselves. Trócaire's emergency response to the Burma cyclone provided lifesaving food supplies for 350,000 people and was distributed through local church workers. Church networks throughout the country can raise funds quickly by asking organisations and groups in local churches and schools for help.

Long-term aid (for development)

These organisations also work to help people to help themselves in the long-term. There is a saying, 'Give a man a fish and he can feed himself for a day, give him a fishing rod and you feed him for a lifetime'. Development work brings about long-term changes to communities in need by improving access to drinking water and sanitation, education and tools, and providing initial investments in some 'start-up' local businesses, such as farms to help communities help themselves. Long-term development is important because it empowers people and enables them to regain a sense of their own dignity and self-respect and the ability to support themselves.

Extension activity

Using these organisations' websites, research how each charity campaigns for and supports women's rights or people living with HIV/Aids.

Activities

1   Identify as many different aspects of the work of Christian aid agencies from the quotations as you can. Imagine you are a worker for one of these charities. Produce a poster to appeal to Christians to give more and get involved. Think carefully about the audience you want to appeal to – adults, people of your age or younger children.

2   What links can you make between Christian beliefs and the work of these charities?

3   Explain the difference between emergency aid and long-term development aid.

Study tip

Make sure you can give specific examples of the different kinds of work the charities undertake.

Summary

You should now be able to explain the difference between emergency aid and long-term development work and show how organisations such as Christian Aid, Tearfund, Trócaire, and CAFOD work for the poor overseas.

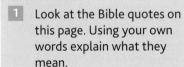

6.3 Pacifism

Christian pacifism

Pacifism is the belief that violent acts are wrong and that only peaceful, non-violent solutions to disagreement should ever be used. Biblical teachings suggest that peace is a better way forward.

These teachings and others have led some Christians to dedicate themselves against acts of violence, no matter what the justification. These Churches are sometimes referred to as Peace Churches.

Different kinds of pacifism

Different Christian pacifists understand pacifism in different ways:

A

Violence allowed for personal defence, not warfare	The use of coercion and/or force or violence may be acceptable for purposes of personal self-defence but resorting to warfare is not an option open to Christians.
Neutrality (refusing to get involved in military conflict)	Jehovah's Witnesses believe that no one who follows God has any right to lay down his life on behalf of the state – this constitutes idolatry. Jehovah's Witnesses hold a position of neutrality and maintained that position during the Second World War.
Non-violence (a strong pacifist position rejecting all violence)	The Fellowship of Reconciliation brings together Christian pacifists from different Churches and in the United Kingdom it is an organisation of Christian non-violence.
Non-combatancy (refusal to be involved in military combat)	The Seventh-day Adventist Church took a position in 1867 of non-combatancy (not supporting combat) with regards to military service. Church members may choose combat but the Church stands by its official position.

The Quakers

The **Quakers** are an important example of Christians who reject all forms of violence.

> 66 We utterly deny all outward wars and strife, and fightings with outward weapons, for any end, or under any pretence whatever; this is our testimony to the whole world … [W]e certainly know, and testify to the world, that the Spirit of Christ, which leads us into all truth, will never move us to fight and war against any man with outward weapons, neither for the kingdom of Christ, nor for the kingdoms of this world. 99
>
> *Quaker Declaration*

During the First World War, Quakers and other pacifists supported people who refused to join the army because of their religious or ethical beliefs. They were often given dangerous tasks.

- For instance, they were sometimes assigned as stretcher-bearers, sent out onto the battlefields to bring in the dead and wounded.
- In the Second World War Christian pacifists drove ambulances during the London Blitz. They were called the Friends' Ambulance Unit. They would drive with their headlamps off (because of the blackout) towards the sights and sounds of the bombings and into the bombing areas to search for the injured. They also travelled abroad to places where troops were fighting and provided first aid and rescue for injured soldiers. They were unarmed.

The Civil Rights Activist and Protestant preacher Dr Martin Luther King Jr also preached non-violence in his work to bring about equality for black Americans.

> 66 The ultimate weakness of violence is that it is a descending spiral, begetting the very thing it seeks to destroy. Instead of diminishing evil, it multiplies it. Through violence you may murder the liar, but you cannot murder the lie, nor establish the truth. Through violence you may murder the hater, but you do not murder hate. In fact, violence merely increases hate. So it goes … Returning hate for hate multiplies hate, adding deeper darkness to a night already devoid of stars. Darkness cannot drive out darkness: only light can do that. Hate cannot drive out hate: only love can do that. 99
>
> *Dr Martin Luther King Jr, Baptist Minister*

The Mennonites

The Mennonite Church grew out of the Protestant Reformation in Europe in the early 1500s. Mennonites believe Christ's instruction to 'love your enemies' means they cannot participate in any way in military action against another.

Gandhi

Many teachers of other religious traditions argue that non-violence should be a means for change. For instance, Mahatma Gandhi struggled for Indian independence from Britain.

> 66 What difference does it make to the dead, the orphans, and the homeless, whether the mad destruction is wrought under the name of totalitarianism [a totally controlling ruler] or the holy name of liberty and democracy? 99
>
> *Mahatma Gandhi*

Activities

2 To what extent do the Bible teachings require Christians to be pacifists? Give reasons for your opinion.

3 Compare the Christian arguments for pacifism with those that are in favour of a just war. Choose the strongest three arguments from each point of view and decide which you find most convincing and why.

4 Which of the different forms of Christian pacifism do you agree with the most and why?

B   Gandhi

> 66 An eye for an eye only makes the whole world blind. 99
>
> *Mahatma Gandhi*

Study tip

Different Christian groups have different degrees of pacifism. Show that you understand some different interpretations of Christian pacifism.

Summary

You should now be able to explain what pacifism is and why some Christians are pacifists. You should be able to discuss and evaluate different arguments about Christian pacifism.

What is terrorism?

Terrorism is defined as the systematic use of terror especially as a means of coercion, that is, forcing people to do something. It usually refers to acts which are:

- violent
- intended to create fear through a psychological impact
- carried out for some ideological or political goal
- deliberately targeted at civilians
- disguised (terrorists frequently disguise themselves and non-combatants so they cannot be identified).

Acts of terror may take a number of forms but frequently include causing explosions, beatings and executions and kidnapping for ransom.

What are the causes of terrorism?

It is difficult to generalise about terrorism. There are many different causes, sometimes very local ones, sometimes national or international. Causes include:

- a grievance – a sense of not having any political influence
- political, social and economic inequality
- economic problems and high unemployment
- religious extremism (very strongly held religious views which do not accept any other views as valid)
- ethnic conflict.

Experts today suggest that each of these factors has a role to play. The most important causes seem to be political power struggles, and people seeing injustice between those who are poor and those who are rich. Any religious and ethnic tensions tend to be used by terrorists to generate support for their cause.

History is filled with examples of terrorism. Until recently, terrorist organisations operated in Northern Ireland and the Republic of Ireland. Nationalist and Unionist terrorist organisations caused explosions and carried out killings among members of each other's communities. Both were politically motivated and culturally and religiously divided.

Terrorism after 9/11 and 7/7

Today terrorism is seen in the light of radical militant Islamist attacks, especially the 9/11 attacks on the World Trade Center in 2001 and the 7/7 attacks on the London transport system in 2005. These attacks were the result of the radicalisation of young Muslims by militant Islamist groups. These groups identify grievances to justify their actions including the Israeli occupation of Palestine and the war in Iraq. This period has also seen the rise of the suicide bomber, a dangerous and difficult threat to prevent. Terrorism now has a global dimension, as many parts of the world are affected.

Key terms

Terrorism: when groups use violence, or the threat of violence, to achieve their aims, rather than using a democratic process. The violence is often indiscriminate, to create maximum fear.

Discussion activity

Can it ever be right to use violence and fear to reach a political objective?

A   *A bomber killed 13 people on this London bus; in total, 52 people were killed in four suicide attacks*

Study tip

You do not need to know Muslim teaching about terrorism for the exam but it is important to remember that Muslim and Christain attitudes to terrorism and to the importance of respect for every human being are very similar.

⊙⊙links

Look back at Chapter 1, The sanctity of life, pages 8–9

The teachings of the Qur'an and Muslim responses

- The teachings of the Qur'an, as understood by Muslim scholars and believers, do not and have never permitted the use of suicide bombers or the taking of innocent life.
- The Qur'an upholds the sanctity and dignity of human life. The use of suicide bombers has divided even the militant Islamist groups themselves because terrorism ignores this Muslim teaching.
- Muslims living in Christian or secular countries believe they must live by the laws of that land as well as by the laws of their faith.

War on Terror?

Some believe that as a result of these attacks, a war on terror must be waged throughout the world wherever this kind of terrorism grows. This includes the NATO invasion of Afghanistan, the American and British invasion of Iraq (which some argue was illegal and unjust), and other military and political activities throughout the world.

Others argue that this is not a war of civilisations or a war at all. The language of war suggests the fighters are soldiers but in fact they are only criminals.

The threat to the community

This form of terrorism threatens a number of aspects of community life.

- Members of the Muslim communities are fearful that they will be seen in the same terms as the radical militant Islamists, causing greater divisions in society.
- Governments, worried about terrorism, restrict freedoms in an attempt to protect the public.
- The terrorists themselves spread fear as well as injury and death through their actions.

Christian responses to terrorism

The overwhelming majority of all Christians and Churches oppose terrorism. Christians believe that terrorism:

- prevents reconciliation between different peoples
- aggravates problems and tensions
- leads to suffering and harm.

Christian responses to terrorism indicate that, even if force is necessary against terrorism, it is essential both to address the causes of terrorism and to promote respect for every human being and the unity of humanity.

> We share the deep anger toward those who so callously and massively destroy innocent lives, no matter what the grievances or injustices invoked. In the name of God, we too demand that those responsible for these utterly evil acts be found and brought to justice. Those culpable must not escape accountability. But we must not, out of anger and vengeance, indiscriminately retaliate in ways that bring on even more loss of innocent life.
>
> From a statement signed by hundreds of Christian leaders and representatives from other faith communities after the 9/11 attacks

Summary

You should now be able to explain what terrorism is and what might cause it. You should also know how Christians respond to terrorism.

Extension activity

'Preventing violent extremism – toolkit for schools' is a government-led initiative to encourage schools and communities. Find out more about it on the internet at **http://www.teachernet.gov.uk/wholeschool/violentextremism/** and work in a group, perhaps with teachers and teaching assistants, to discuss what sorts of things could be done in school to help younger children live and work better together.

6.5　　Nuclear warfare and proliferation

◼ Dropping the atom bomb

In 1945 America dropped two atomic bombs over Japan: the first over the city of Hiroshima and the second over the city of Nagasaki. Over 140,000 people were killed instantly. Many more were horrifically injured. Pregnant women gave birth to severely deformed babies. Many developed cancers as a direct result of the radiation they were exposed to. In the decades after, many more continued to die of related illnesses. The power of these two bombs forced Japan to surrender and opened a new chapter of human warfare. Today's nuclear weapons are far more powerful than those two bombs.

A *Nuclear blast*

Key terms

Nuclear war: a war in which the participants use nuclear weapons.

Nuclear proliferation: the increase in the number of states that have the potential to use nuclear weapons.

Discussion activity ●●●

If it is possible to end a war quickly by dropping a nuclear bomb on a city, could it be justified?

◼ The arms race

After the Second World War, many other countries became nuclear powers including Britain, the Soviet Union, France, China, Israel, South Africa, Pakistan, India and North Korea. America and the Soviet Union in the 1960s, 70s and 80s built many nuclear weapons, each trying to keep pace with the other.

Many Christians are deeply opposed to this arms race. If there was a **nuclear war** the destruction would be terrible. There would be instant blindness for anyone looking at the flash. Everything within a few miles of the bomb would be incinerated. Hundred-mile-an-hour winds would flatten everything over a much greater area. Radioactive fallout would contaminate everything for tens, even hundreds of miles. The radiation would remain for decades, perhaps longer, and any who survived would have slow, lingering deaths from radiation.

B   *Hiroshima. Ground Zero for the first atomic bomb.*

Extension activity

The Cuban Missile Crisis is perhaps the closest the world has come to total nuclear war. Use the internet to find out more about it.

Activity

1   Explain what is meant by total war or nuclear holocaust, nuclear war, nuclear proliferation, and deterrence.

Study tip

While it is not necessary for you to know the history of nuclear weapons for the exam, it is important that you understand the issues to do with them.

The fear of nuclear war was so great that many children growing up at the height of the Cold War in the 1960s–1980s suffered nightmares about nuclear war. Many people became opposed to nuclear weapons because of the devastation to the cities in Japan and the much greater threat they presented to the world.

Nuclear proliferation

Nuclear proliferation means the increase in countries which have nuclear weapons. The more countries that have nuclear weapons, the more likely it is that they will be used again. Terrorist organisations may one day have enough money to buy them or might steal them. The proliferation of nuclear weapons makes the world a more dangerous place.

Activity

2   Based on what you know already, how do you think Christians will respond to the issues surrounding nuclear proliferation and deterrence.

Deterrence

When the United States and the Soviet Union were both superpowers there was a belief called Mutually Agreed Destruction (MAD): as long as both sides were convinced that using nuclear weapons would cause the complete destruction of both countries, neither would ever use their nuclear weapons. During the Cuban Missile Crisis in 1968 a dispute between America and the Soviet Union over the placement of missiles in communist Cuba almost led to such a conflict, but not quite. It is argued that the peace between the US and the Soviet Union depended on the presence of the threat of nuclear war and therefore that nuclear weapons were a necessary evil. But what is the situation when many countries and political groupings have nuclear weapons? Do nuclear weapons still ensure peace for fear of something worse?

Summary

You should now be able to explain the dangers of nuclear weapons and nuclear proliferation.

6.6 Christian responses to nuclear warfare and proliferation

Christian responses to nuclear weapons

The vast majority of Christian Churches oppose the mass destructive power of nuclear weapons and its impact on civilian populations, communities, cities and societies. Some argue it is difficult to imagine any situation when a just war could be fought with nuclear weapons because they could never be used in a proportionate way.

> **Objective**
>
> Consider Christian arguments for and against the use and possession of nuclear weapons.

> *There are no nuclear weapons on the island of Ireland and we would find them unacceptable.*
>
> Daniel Newsam of the Church of Ireland

> *There is no ethical justification for weapons of mass destruction – Christian, Muslim, Jewish or humanist – no more than for the suicide bomber.*
>
> Canon Dr Paul Oestreicher – Church of England

> **Discussion activity**
>
> 'Nuclear weapons are the greatest evil made by man; they are the opposite of the Creator God.'
>
> 'To protect yourself in the modern world you need a terrible last resort.'
>
> Consider these two opinions. What do you think?

> *The Roman Catholic Church is totally opposed to nuclear weapons. The Scottish Catholic hierarchy has produced documents condemning the possession of nuclear weapons, not just their use; possession of them is immoral, as to use them remains a temptation.*
>
> Mario Conti, the Roman Catholic Archbishop of Glasgow

> *In this age, which boasts of its atomic power, it no longer makes sense to maintain that war is a fit instrument with which to repair the violation of justice.*
>
> Pope John XXIII, Pacem in Terris ('Peace on Earth')

> *Mankind must put an end to war before war puts an end to mankind.*
>
> John F. Kennedy

Christian responses to the deterrence argument

Some Christians consider the deterrence argument only to be acceptable as a step towards disarmament.

> *In current conditions 'deterrence' based on balance, certainly not as an end in itself but as a step on the way toward a progressive disarmament, may still be judged morally acceptable. Nonetheless in order to ensure peace, it is indispensable not to be satisfied with this minimum which is always susceptible to the real danger of explosion.*
>
> Pope John Paul II, Message to the UN Special Session (1982) 3

A 'Buy one get one free. Everything must go.'

> *Christians should make common cause in supporting international attempts to limit the proliferation of arms. Nuclear weapons are the most urgent priority.*
>
> *The Methodist Church of Great Britain*

Nuclear disarmament

Since the 1950s the Campaign for Nuclear Disarmament (CND) and others have worked for nuclear disarmament. Many Christians have been involved in this campaign and many people would like to see all nuclear weapons destroyed.

In 1963 the Catholic Church called for multilateral disarmament. That means that all countries should destroy all their weapons. This position was repeated recently:

> *The truth of peace requires that all agree to change their course by clear and firm decisions, and strive for a progressive and concerted nuclear disarmament.*
>
> *Pope Benedict XVI, in his* Message for the World Day for Peace, *2007*

Some Christians have gone further and suggest that countries should unilaterally disarm (get rid of their own weapons and not worry about waiting for others to go first). Britain's nuclear weapons systems are ageing and the government has decided to replace them with more nuclear weapons. The government feels there is a need to continue to have a nuclear defence. Churches including the Methodist Church have expressed their disagreement.

The Church of England has suggested that keeping nuclear weapons as a defensive option simply encourages proliferation:

> *The Conference opposes replacement of the Trident nuclear weapons system and urges the UK Government to take leadership in disarmament negotiations in order to bring about the intention of the Non-Proliferation Treaty for the elimination of all nuclear weapons.*
>
> *Methodist Conference, 2006*

> *The debate on nuclear weapons needs to be conducted with much greater honesty and consistency. If certain countries retain their nuclear weapons on the basis of the uncertainty and potentially violent volatility of international relations, on what basis are the same weapons denied to other states? The non-nuclear weapon states need to be presented with rather more convincing arguments and incentives than they have been up to now as to why it might be in their best, long-term interests not to go nuclear.*
>
> *Synod Working Party, 2003*

Activities

1. Outline arguments for and against a country keeping nuclear weapons.

2. Could possession of nuclear weapons be justified on the grounds of the Just War Theory?

3. List as many clear arguments (Christian and otherwise) for and against the government's decision to renew Britain's nuclear weapons system. Add reasons to justify each of the arguments. Identify the three strongest arguments for the decision and the three strongest arguments against the decision, including a Christian argument for both sides, and use this information for a debate or discussion.

Extension activity

CND, the Campaign for Nuclear Disarmament has been working for the elimination of nuclear weapons for decades. Find out more about the organisation using the internet.

Study tip

While many Christians are opposed to nuclear war, there are differences in their opinions about what should be done with the nuclear weapons which already exist. Make sure you can explain those differences.

Summary

You should now be able to discuss different Christian responses to the possession and use of nuclear weapons.

6.7 The causes of crime

■ What is crime?

Crime is the breaking of a law established by a government for which there is a punishment. Crime includes: acts of violence, burglary, vandalism, vehicle-related theft and vandalism, sexual offences, drug offences, fraud and forgery and criminal damage.

■ What are the causes of crime?

Economic, social and family factors

Crime has many causes. Some are economic – a lack of money or opportunities to get a job or decent housing. Some are social/environmental:

A *Causes of crime*

Economic	Social environmental	Family
• Lack of financial resources can lead to poverty. • Lack of educational opportunities can lead to poor work opportunities and housing.	• Prevalence of drugs. • Inequality. • Lack of support for families. • Belief that there are no services available. • Lack of leadership in communities. • Low value placed on children or individual well being. • Gang culture.	• Dysfunctional family conditions. • Substance abuse in the family (drugs or alcohol). • Violence in the family.

Christian perspectives on crime

Christians may agree with the root social, economic and family causes of crime but, in addition, they might suggest some other factors:

■ Moral failings: partly because of original sin, human beings are flawed and are more likely to be sinful; for instance, selfishness and greed can lead to crimes.

■ Evil or the devil: the Devil or Satan may be actively influencing people and causing crime.

■ What impact does crime have on society?

There is a great deal of speculation about the level of crime in society. In recent years levels of crime have decreased in the UK though some violent crimes have increased and fear of crime has increased. Some people are more likely to be a victim of crime. Young men are the most likely, followed by students and unemployed people.

The effects of crime

Crime has short- and long-term effects:

■ Crime can cost people their lives.

■ Medical costs, property losses, and loss of income (for instance, if someone is unable to work because of crime).

Objectives

Explore the causes and effects of crime.

Consider Christian responses to crime.

Key terms

Crime: breaking the law.

Discussion activity ●●●

Is a crime involving violence against a person more serious than a crime which takes resources away from public services, such as theft of medicines from a hospital? Give reasons for your answer.

Activities

1. 'These causes are wrong. Not all poor people are criminals. Not all children from difficult family situations are criminals. Everyone has a choice and sometimes people make the wrong choice and we should not make excuses for them.' To what extent do you think this is true? Give reasons for your view.

2. Why do you think there is so much crime in society?

3. There are many crimes committed by young people against young people. Why do you think this is and what effect does it have?

- Crime can affect all aspects of a person's life and often leaves the victim experiencing anxiety, depression or in some cases post traumatic disorders.
- People can suffer a fear of crime which may mean they feel they cannot go out and enjoy life.
- The trauma of crime can be felt by friends and can disrupt family life.
- Society at large pays for individual crimes through rising costs of security (stronger locks, extra lighting, security alarms, etc.) and general anxiety.

How do Christians respond to crime?

The values of the Beatitudes and the Commandments present a clear message towards crime (Exodus 20:2–14; Matthew 5:3–12). They emphasise fairness, honesty and justice:

- Live a life based on love of neighbour and love of God, not pursuing own selfish interests.
- Do not take or covet what is not yours (commandments).
- Be honest in your dealings – do not lie (commandment).
- Be an upholder of justice ('Blessed are those who hunger for righteousness', 'Blessed are the pure in heart').
- Respect the value of human life ('Do not kill', 'Blessed are the peacemakers').

These teachings and values suggest that Christianity does not tolerate crime. Crime undermines society and family life and encourages selfish individualist attitudes.

When might Christians challenge the law?

Protest against the law

The great teacher of the Church, St Thomas Aquinas, once said that a law that is an unjust law is no law at all. In other words, he recognised that there could be a situation where the law of the land encouraged immoral activity and should not be followed. A Christian's duty to bring about a just world means they have to act against injustice. For instance:

- if it encouraged paying certain people lower wages because they were black
- if it did not uphold the rights of workers, women, or the disabled.

Breaking the law

Look at the case study of a Christian who acted against the law. There are more common situation's where Christians might consider there to be conflict in duties. Consider the example in Activity 4.

- There are other, more common situations, where Christians might consider there to be a conflict in duties. For instance, might it be justified to steal if you are starving? Should you pay taxes to your government if they are doing things you consider immoral? Consider the example in the Discussion activity.

Activity

4   A rich tourist from a rich country is walking through a market on holiday in a desperately poor country. He has a $10 bill sticking out of his pocket, four months' wages in this country. A boy from a family on the edge of starvation and sickness, sees the note and picks the man's pocket. He takes the note home and is able to buy food and medicines for his family. Identify the Christian arguments for and against the boy's action. Decide which argument is stronger, on Christian grounds.

Case study

There are stories of courageous Christians who, motivated by conscience, demonstrated and protested against inequalities, sometimes at the cost of their own lives. Some Christians campaign against things they see as wrong in this society.

Dietrich Bonhoffer, a famous Protestant Pastor and theologian, and a pacifist, was involved in the plot to assassinate Hitler. Clearly the Bible forbids killing and assassination was illegal in Germany, but Bonhoffer felt moved to go against this teaching and the law in this particular instance.

Study tip

There are many biblical teachings which relate to crime. Make sure you can link these teachings with Christian attitudes towards crime.

Summary

You should now be able to discuss the causes and effects of crime and different Christians' responses to law breaking.

6.8　The aims of punishment

Why do we punish people?

Retribution
This means revenge for what has been done against the laws of society or the individual.

Deterrence
As a warning to others to try to discourage them from committing the same crime.

The aims of punishment

Reformation
Crime prevention, rehabilitation, education, substance abuse treatment and reintegration programmes are essential to make punishment effective by changing behaviours.

Protection
Protecting society by stopping the individual criminals from being able to commit crimes against people, typically through prison, or some other restriction on a person's movement such as by electronic tagging.

 A *Aims of punishment*

Christian responses

For Christians these social aims are understood from a religious perspective.

Retribution, justice and restoration

Some find parts of the Bible that suggest some degree of **retribution** or possibly restoration:

> 66 *If anyone injures his neighbour, whatever he has done, must be done to him: fracture for fracture, eye for eye, tooth for tooth. As he has injured the other so he is to be injured.* 99
>
> *Leviticus* 24:19–20

In fact this text was interpreted in Jesus' time as meaning that some payment would be made equivalent to the injury or loss caused. Some Christians use this to justify quite strict dealings with criminals.

Justice is an important part of Christian values expressed in the Beatitudes (Matthew 5), but Jesus rejected punishment for its own sake as we are all sinners (John 8). The idea of restoring, or 'setting right' is an important Christian idea:

> 66 *A Catholic approach leads us to encourage models of restorative justice that seek to address crime in terms of the harm done to victims and communities, not simply as a violation of law.* 99
>
> *A Statement of the Catholic Bishops of the United States*

Objectives

Explore different aims and forms of punishment.

Explain Christian beliefs about forgiveness and non-retaliation with regard to punishment.

Key terms

Retribution: to 'get your own back' on the criminal, based on the Old Testament teaching of 'an eye for an eye'. An aim of punishment aimed at being proportionate to the offence committed.

Reform: to change someone's behaviour for the better. An aim of punishment.

Deterrence: to put people off committing crimes. One of the aims of punishment.

Protection: to stop the criminal hurting anyone in society. An aim of punishment.

Activities

1　Why do we punish? To get back at the person, in reparation for what was done, to deter others, to protect others, or to reform the criminal?

2　What might a Christian believe punishment should be about?

Extension activity

Jesus was sometimes very concerned about the nature of the punishment being given to people. Read John 8:1–11. It gives an account of a woman on trial for adultery in the Temple court. Write down what you think it suggests about Jesus' attitude towards punishment and methods of punishment.

Reform and rehabilitation

For Christians the belief in the possibility of redemption through the grace of God is important.

> *No-one is totally defined by their sins and failures, and the image of God in all human beings relates to potentiality as well as actuality.*
>
> *Church of England Report*

Jesus came to heal the sick, and criminals who act immorally, or sinfully by harming others through what they do, need to change to realise that they should love God and their neighbour:

> *Christians must look for ways of dealing with crime that hold out hope for both offenders and victims.*
>
> *Church of England Report*

Deterrence

Deterrence is a biblical idea:

> *For rulers hold no terror for those who do right, but for those who do wrong. Do you want to be free from fear of the one in authority? Then do what is right and he will commend you. For he is God's servant to do you good. But if you do wrong, be afraid, for he does not bear the sword for nothing. He is God's servant, an agent of wrath to bring punishment on the wrongdoer.*
>
> *Romans 13:3–4*

Protection

For many Christians the teaching to love your neighbour would also include helping to **protect** them from danger. Just as the good Samaritan helps the man who has been robbed and beaten by bandits, so people in society should be protected from those who pose a threat to them.

■ Punishment and forgiveness

Jesus' teaching on punishment and forgiveness may seem incredible by today's standards.

Beliefs and teachings

'You have heard that it was said, "Eye for eye, and tooth for tooth." But I tell you, Do not resist an evil person. If someone strikes you on the right cheek, turn to him the other also.'

Matthew 5:38–39

'Do not judge, or you too will be judged.'

Matthew 7:1

The emphasis on forgiveness is in keeping with Christian teaching about the importance of forgiveness (see the parable of the Forgiving Father). Forgiving others was central to Jesus' life, he even asked God to forgive as he was dying on the cross. This extended to not retaliating against crimes done. Retribution does not seem to be upheld by the Gospel message, even though it seems to be part of the Old Testament teaching.

Discussion activities

'Sometimes people do things so terrible that they should be locked up and we should throw away the key.'

'It is easier to think of those who have committed serious crimes as monsters, than face the reality that, given their life experiences, we may have gone exactly the same way.'

'The good of the many outweigh the good of the few, so we should play safe and keep criminals inside.'

'If we decide that some people can never be forgiven then there is no hope for any of us.'

'Why bother trying to reform people who have done terrible things? They had their chance. They should suffer.'

1 Discuss which of these quotes you most strongly agree or disagree with.

2 Decide which you think reflect Christian teachings more closely, and justify your answer.

> *'Why do you look at the speck of sawdust in your brother's eye and pay no attention to the plank in your own eye?'*
>
> *Matthew 7:3*

Study tip

Remember you need to be able to give specific Christian responses to questions about punishment.

Summary

You should now be able to explain different aims of punishment and different Christian responses.

The impact of punishment

How do we punish people?

In the past punishments tended to be physically brutal and severe. Theft of food could lead to long imprisonment. Many villages had stocks where **offenders** might be chained to be ridiculed.

Today punishment usually restricts a person's freedom. Recently the UK has increased the number of crimes leading to a prison sentence and so prison numbers have risen. It is also the case that many people in prison suffer from mental health illnesses and many have very poor educational levels.

As well as **imprisonment** and **community service** there are other forms of punishment including fines, for instance for driving offences, and more limited forms of restriction such as electronic tagging and probation.

> **Objectives**
>
> Explore arguments for and against some forms of punishment.
>
> Examine how punishment affects individuals, communities and society.

> **Key terms**
>
> **Offender**: someone who has done wrong, e.g. broken the law.

Arguments about methods of punishment

A

Method	For	Against
Imprisonment More serious crimes such as violent assault, rape and murder bring prison sentences. The restriction of a person's freedom is both a punishment and also protects the community while the person is in prison. It may also allow for reform if there are education facilities available.	■ Prison stops people from committing more crimes and so protects society. ■ Long prison sentences are a deterrent for more serious crimes.	■ Prisons are overcrowded, educational facilities are poor so prisoners are not reformed. ■ A majority of prisoners re-offend after they have been released. Prison does not protect society in the long run. ■ We send more people to prison than ever before but crime levels are high. It is not much of a deterrent. ■ Prisons are academies of crime for new criminals to learn from more experienced criminals and develop drug dependencies.
Fines	■ Taking money from the offender is a deterrent. ■ The money raised can be used for society as a whole and to help victims.	■ For the rich the fine has little deterrence. ■ For the poor the fine could be much harder and take money from dependants, such as children.
Probation/Suspended sentence Allowing a (usually) first-time minor offender (the person who committed the crime) not to go to prison but instead to allow them to live life as normal. If a further crime is committed within a set period, then the prison sentence is passed. Sometimes certain conditions on where the person may go and what they may do are added.	■ It gives the minor offender a chance to start to reintegrate into normal life. ■ The offender is provided with some support, usually a probation officer, who monitors and helps them to start to lead a normal life, reducing the likelihood of re-offending.	■ It gives offenders the chance to harm people again, or themselves. ■ It does not send the 'right' message to other criminals that crime does not pay, and does not deter them.
Community service Community service refers to forced work for the community such as cleaning, tending to public gardens or other forms of work for the public good. This is a more public act of reparation for the crime committed. The public are able to see the criminal working for what they have done wrong.	■ It actually requires the offender to do something for the community that he/she has harmed. ■ It provides them with an opportunity to do something productive which may help them begin to change their lives. ■ It is more effective for lesser crimes than imprisonment.	■ It is a soft option which does not cause much real discomfort to the offender. ■ It is nothing to fear, so does not act as a deterrent.

▮ The effect of punishment on society

Is prison the best option?

In the 19th century, Elizabeth Fry, a Quaker Christian campaigned that prisons should be humane. The prisons at that time were terrible places but people are still concerned today. The Prison Reform Trust argues that prisons are the most shaming of all our public institutions. The UK has the highest imprisonment rate in Western Europe at 145 per 100,000 of the population. They argue that conditions in UK prisons are often an affront to civilised values, and at great cost to the taxpayer. However, the vast majority of UK prisoners do not present a serious threat to life or limb. The Prison Reform Trust argues that many crimes can be more humanely, economically and effectively dealt with in the community. Not all prisons need to be high security and, indeed, some are 'open prisons' suitable for less serious criminals.

Who is affected by punishment?

While it is obvious that the person punished is directly affected by the form of punishment, there are others who are also affected, indirectly.

Consider:

- A father of two, serving a life imprisonment for murder. What will be the impact on his children and wife?
- A 15-year-old girl serving a short period in a youth offender institute (for criminals too young to go to prison or be treated as an adult criminal) for a violent assault. What will be the impact on her family and friends?

NO TO WAR
NOT IN MY NAME
NO
Resist
Revolt
MAB
DON'T ATTACK IRAQ

6.10 The death penalty

The death penalty across the world

The death penalty, or **capital punishment**, is the execution of a criminal by the government. According to Amnesty International in 2006, 1,591 people were executed in 25 countries and at least 3,861 people were sentenced to death in 55 countries. In 2007, 24 countries executed 1,252 people (88 per cent of whom were in China, Iran, Pakistan, Saudi Arabia, and the United States alone). There are over 20,000 prisoners on 'death row' across the world.

Objectives

Examine arguments for and against the death penalty.

Explore Christian responses to the death penalty.

Key terms

Capital punishment: form of punishment in which a prisoner is put to death for crimes committed.

Discussion activities

1. Should we only execute people for the most terrible or multiple murders?
2. Should we execute people for crimes such as violent rape, terrorism and drug trafficking?
3. Should we execute people for committing murder?
4. Is the death penalty worse than imprisoning someone for life?
5. Should a Christian oppose the death penalty in all situations?

In total, 137 countries have abolished the death penalty either in law or in practice and 69 other countries retain and use the death penalty. In a 2008 poll, 99 per cent of almost 100,000 the *Sun* newspaper readers voted in favour of a return to the death penalty. One voter said 'They took away their victims' human rights and gave up theirs when they committed their hideous crimes. Bring back hanging, I say' (the *Sun*, 25 February 2008).

Arguments for and against the death penalty

A The death penalty

B

Arguments for the death penalty	Arguments against the death penalty
■ It permanently removes the worst criminals, leaving society safer. ■ It would be cheaper than incarcerating a person for life. ■ It offers retribution, a life for a life. ■ Fear of the death penalty may deter other potential killers. In Singapore, which often carries out death sentences, there is far less serious crime. ■ If someone murders someone else, they have given up their human rights, including the one to stay alive themselves. ■ It 'fits the crime' of murder – if you have killed, you should be killed as well. ■ The most serious criminals only understand the language of violence.	■ It contradicts the most basic human right to life. ■ It can be torturously painful. ■ Some countries with the death penalty have higher rates of murder than those without the death penalty – it doesn't seem to deter. ■ Innocent people will be executed by mistake. It may be that a person has killed someone, but perhaps only in self-defence, for instance. ■ The families and friends of those waiting for the death penalty, who are innocent, have to go through terrible trauma. Why should they suffer? ■ The presence of the death penalty in society may have a brutalising effect, causing people to show less respect for the dignity of the human person. ■ There are alternatives to the death penalty, such as life imprisonment which may give the opportunity for someone to change.

'Jesus wants Christians to stand up for the weak. As Christians we have a duty to protect the weak in society and sometimes that means removing the most terrible criminals. The death penalty does this.'

'As a Christian I believe that all killing is wrong. God said so in the Commandments.'

'The Old Testament says an eye for an eye, a tooth for tooth.'

'Jesus was executed himself. I don't believe he would want us to keep executing prisoners.'

'In the Beatitudes Jesus taught that we should uphold justice, that must mean upholding punishments.'

'Jesus taught that we should love our enemies and forgive the sins of others. The death penalty cannot be either of these?'

'God wants all people to understand that they have sinned and seek forgiveness. If we execute them we take away the possibility of this.'

1   Consider these Christian perspectives, and use them for a discussion.

C   Is life imprisonment more or less humane than execution?

Remember that you must be able to explain Christian attitudes to the death penalty, not simply general arguments for or against.

Christian responses to the death penalty

D   Christian news on the death penalty

The death penalty is necessary only in rare cases	God has authorised the death penalty
'The traditional teaching of the church does not exclude recourse to the death penalty, if this is the only possible way of effectively defending human lives against the unjust aggressor' (Catechism 2267). **The death penalty undermines the sanctity of life** Many Christians are deeply opposed to the death penalty in any situation because of a deep commitment to the sanctity of all human life and a belief in the commandments 'do not kill' and the teaching 'love your neighbour'. **The death penalty brutalises society** 'Capital punishment feeds the cycle of violence in society by pandering to a lust for revenge. It brutalises us, and deadens our sensitivities to the precious nature of every single human life'. (Most Rev. David B. Thompson, Bishop of Charleston, SC, 3 December 1998). 'We cannot teach that killing is wrong by killing' (US Catholic Bishops, 1994).	The Old Testament lists crimes which can be punished by the death penalty. Barrett Duke, speaking to the Southern Baptists Church in 2000 said that: 'Historically, Southern Baptists have supported capital punishment in our rank and file' and that support for the death penalty: 'is a biblical position. And we do believe that the Bible continues to be relevant for life today. … We do acknowledge that the state has the right to execute those who have violated certain laws. God authorised capital punishment for murder after the Noahic Flood, validating its legitimacy in human society. … Messengers [delegates of the SBC] support the fair and equitable use of capital punishment by civil magistrates as a legitimate form of punishment for those guilty of murder or treasonous acts that result in death' (Southern Baptist Church's year 2000 assembly).

2   What is capital punishment?

3   Suggest three strong arguments in favour of capital punishment and three strong arguments against capital punishment.

4   Explain two different Christian responses to capital punishment.

Amnesty International and Human Rights Watch are organisations which are very concerned about the death penalty. Using the internet, find out more information about current concerns which these organisations have.

You should now be able to suggest arguments for and against the death penalty with reasons to support them, and explain different Christian responses.

Assessment guidance

6

Conflict – summary

For the examination you should now be able to:

✓ explain the terms war, peace, Just War Theory, pacifism, terrorism, nuclear warfare, nuclear proliferation

✓ outline the Just War Theory

✓ describe and explain different Christian attitudes to war

✓ explain Christian attitudes to pacifism

✓ understood the causes of terrorism and explain Christian responses to terrorism

✓ explain Christian responses to nuclear warfare and nuclear proliferation

✓ explain the terms crime, punishment, reform, retribution, deterrence, protection, death penalty

✓ outline the causes of crime and the aims and forms of punishment

✓ explain Christian responses to different kinds of punishment

✓ explain and evaluate Christian beliefs and attitudes towards the death penalty.

Sample answer

1 Read the following exam question
'Outline the Just War Theory.' *(6 marks)*

2 Read this sample answer

> 'For a war to be just it must have been started in the last resort. Everything else should have been tried first. It should be declared by the government. The war should be for a good reason and it should not go too far. The war should be fought fairly.'

3 With a partner, discuss the sample answer. Do you think there are things that could be added or taken out?

4 How many marks would you give this out of 6? Look at the mark scheme in the Introduction on page 7 (AO1). What are the reasons for the mark you have given?

Practice questions

1 What is meant by the word pacifism? *(2 marks)*

2 Outline four aims of punishment. *(4 marks)*

3 Explain the causes of war. *(6 marks)*

4 'A Christian should always be a pacifist.' Do you agree? Give reasons for your answer,
showing that you have thought about more than one point of view. Refer to Christian
teaching in your answer. *(6 marks)*

Study tip Remember, when you are asked if you agree with a statement, you must show
what you think and the reasons why other people might hold different views.
If your answer is one-sided you will only achieve a maximum of 4 marks. If you
make no religious comment then you will achieve no more than 3 marks.

Glossary

A

Abortion: the deliberate termination (ending) of a pregnancy, usually before the foetus is twenty-four weeks old.

Absolute morality: what is morally right and wrong applies to all circumstances, at all times.

Abuse: misuse of the world and the environment.

Active euthanasia: the ending of a life by a deliberate action, such as by giving a patient a fatal injection.

Adultery: sex outside marriage where at least one of the couple is already married to someone else.

Age of consent: the legal age for sex to be treated as by agreement.

Aid: to help or assist people in need usually by practical assistance and gifts.

Artificial insemination (AI): sperm medically inserted into the vagina to assist pregnancy.

Artificial insemination by donor (AID): when a woman is made pregnant by the sperm of a man other than her partner, but not through having sexual relations with him.

Artificial insemination by husband (AIH): when a woman is made pregnant by the sperm of her husband, but not through having sexual relations with him.

C

CAFOD (Catholic Fund for Overseas Development): a private charity established by the Bishops of England and Wales to bring aid to less economically developed countries.

Capital punishment: form of punishment in which a prisoner is put to death for crimes committed.

Charity: (i) voluntarily giving help, such as money, to those in need; (ii) an organisation set up to help those in need; (iii) Christian love for the needy.

Chastity: sexual purity. Not having sex before marriage.

Christian Aid: a charity working on behalf of the British and Irish churches in combating poverty throughout the world; campaigns under the slogan 'we believe in life before death'.

Civil marriage: non-religious marriage ceremony in a marriage registry office or other licensed venue, e.g. an hotel.

Civil partnership: legal registration and recognition of a same-sex partnership.

Climate change: changes to the climate, believed by some scientists to be irreparably damaging, that have been caused by human lifestyles.

Cloning: the scientific method by which animals or plants can be created which have exactly the same genetic make up as the original, because the DNA of the original is used.

Cohabitation: a couple living together and having a sexual relationship without being married to one another.

Colour: relating to the colour of a person's skin / ethnicity. Often used as a reason for unfairly judging others and making uninformed opinions about them.

Community service: a form of punishment in which the criminal has to perform tasks useful to society, rather than going to prison.

Conservation: looking after the environment and protecting animals.

Conservation projects: projects set up to protect the environment.

Contraception: the artificial and chemical methods used to prevent pregnancy taking place.

Crime: breaking the law.

D

Deterrence: to put people off committing crimes. One of the aims of punishment.

Designer babies: babies with gender and characteristics chosen by their parents – currently illegal.

Disability: when a person has a mental or physical condition that limits movement or activities.

Disability discrimination: acting against someone on the grounds of physical or mental limitations.

Discrimination: to act against someone on the basis of sex, race, religion, etc. Discrimination is usually seen as wrong.

Divorce: legal ending of a marriage.

E

Earth summits: meetings of international leaders aimed at reaching an agreement that will reduce environmental pollution and climate change.

Embryo: fertilised ovum at about 12–14 days when implanted into the wall of the womb.

Embryonic research (embryology): the study of human embryos.

Emergency aid: also known as short-term aid. Help given to communities in a time of disaster or crisis, e.g. food during a famine, shelter after an earthquake.

The environment: a term used to refer to the planet on which we live and its resources.

Environmental conservation: looking after the natural resources of the planet by taking steps to protect them.